CONFRONTING LIFE-THREATENING ILLNESS

Confronting Life-Threatening Illness

Through the Power of Positional Thinking

John E. Packo
the author of *Coping with Cancer*

Christian Publications
3825 Hartzdale Drive, Camp Hill, PA 17011
www.cpi-horizon.com
www.christianpublications.com

Faithful, biblical publishing since 1883

Confronting Life-Threatening Illness
ISBN: 0-87509-935-1
LOC Control Number: 2001-130440

Printed in the United States of America

01 02 03 04 05 5 4 3 2 1

Dedication

I DEDICATE THIS BOOK to my family with love and appreciation for their devotion and support: first, to my mother, who worked hard to bring up six children with her soft-spoken wisdom; second, to my wife, Elaine, for her patience during the long hours of writing this book along with her suggestions for improving it; third, to my sons and their wives, Stephen and Glenda, David and Marilyn and their children. Many thanks also to Glenda for her long hours in correcting and refining the manuscript along with Stephen's suggestions. We all belong to the family of God and give Him the glory for saving us and giving us a seat in the heavenly realms with Christ.

Contents

Foreword

C*onfronting Life-Threatening Illness* is an expanded treatment of the "Seventh Creative Choice" in my book, *Coping with Cancer: 12 Creative Choices*, which is published by Christian Publications, Inc. The "Seventh Creative Choice" states, "I practice positional thinking that produces power to live above tough circumstances." It would be helpful for persons suffering chronic or life-threatening diseases to read the book. It proposes twelve creative choices for meeting any illness head-on with God!

The practice of positional thinking has guided my thoughts through eighteen years of cancer-free living, during which physicians at the University of Michigan declared, "You are a miracle!" I'm grateful to the Lord for healing me, since six months earlier the diagnosis had been, "You have advanced lymphoma with less than one month to live."

Since my miraculous recovery from cancer, I begin my day by praying, "Lord Jesus, thank You for Your death, resurrection and ascension for me. I count my old self to be dead with Your death and my new self to be alive through Your resurrection. As I take my seat with You in the heavenlies, I claim Your resurrection power for this day." This has been an ongoing process in my daily spiritual renewal. It has helped me for years to experience resurrection power over tough circumstances with joyful victory!

Preface

C*onfronting Life-Threatening Illness* is built around a key concept that every believer should understand and practice—the power of positional thinking. There is marvelous, supernatural power in thinking correctly about life's vicissitudes in light of the believer's position in Jesus Christ.

John Packo fully understands that when Jesus Christ rose from the dead, tremendous spiritual power became available to us. He also understands how Christ's present (and positional) authority at the right hand of the Father may profoundly impact our lives.

This book will find its way into a genre of books that includes *Destined for the Throne* by Paul Billheimer and *The Authority of the Believer* by J.A. MacMillan. From its pages, you may properly expect new understandings of your position in Christ.

Frankly, reading this book multiple times has the potential of profoundly changing your life.

K. Neill Foster/Publisher
Christian Publications, Inc.
March 2001

Introduction

Are you going through a tough circumstance? Are you sick, feeling depressed, having bad days? Going through hard times has been the experience of humanity since Adam and Eve's expulsion from the Garden of Eden.

Did you know that Satan wants you crushed and defeated? Are you aware that our old sinful nature is the main avenue through which he operates? Unfortunately, many believers are struggling under the weight of their illnesses and tough circumstances through ignorance. They are unaware of the spiritual warfare being waged against them in the heavens and they don't know how to exercise their power of positional thinking.

This book will show you God's way to victory through the power of positional thinking. It will teach you what the power of positional thinking is. And it will show you how to escape the crushing weight of your tough circumstances and rise above with the joy of victory!

This is a spiritual warfare book. It focuses on the Lord Jesus Christ and our position in Him. I relate some of my experiences of seeing satanic intrusion into the lives of others. Some found deliverance and freedom, but others did not. You will discover why they didn't succeed.

However, this book deals mainly with how positional thinking helps us win the battle against Satan, who is trying to defeat us spiritually, especially when we are ill or are facing some other tough circumstance. Each chapter begins with a summary of the content called *The Positional Thinker's Action*, and a quotation which will challenge the reader. These challenges are placed at the end of the book in the form of *Positional Thinker's Action Cards*. They can be cut out and carried in your pocket or purse and referred to when needed.

Confronting Life-Threatening Illness develops its material in six areas:

1. The first chapter explains the authority of the believer and how spiritual power gives the believer hope in tough circumstances.
2. The second chapter shows how positional thinking differs from positive thinking, and also how the believer rests in the victory already won by Christ on the cross.
3. The next three chapters explain that the basis of spiritual power in tough circumstances is Christ's death, resurrection and ascension.
4. Chapter 6 presents testing of the spirits, which may be used to determine whether or not information is from God.
5. In chapters 7-9, six powerful weapons that defeat destructive thinking are presented, along with an explanation of how positional thinkers apply them in tough circumstances.
6. Chapters 10-13 describe twenty-four arrows of physical, social, spiritual and psychological damage and explain how the positional thinker deals with

them. Among other things, we will learn how Satan uses illnesses to defeat us.

The powers of this dark world and the spiritual forces of evil in the heavenly realms are bent on destroying the believer's active spiritual life. The Christian, however, has the advantage of an authoritative position in the heavenly realms. Jesus, through His death, resurrection and ascension, has broken the power of Satan and our old sinful nature. He has raised us to an authoritative position of positive strength and assurance.

The old serpent wants you to feel depressed, get sick and have bad days every day! Don't give him that satisfaction. Read this book. Practice positional thinking and learn how to use your authority as you move through your tough circumstances.

"I practice positional thinking that produces power to live above tough circumstances."

ONE

Positional Power Brings Authority to the Believer

. . . that you may know the hope to which he has called you, the riches of his glorious inheritance in the saints, and his incomparably great power for us who believe. That power is like the working of his mighty strength, which he exerted in Christ when he raised him from the dead and seated him at his right hand in the heavenly realms. (Ephesians 1:18-20)

Enormous power is necessary for spiritual warfare. It takes the power of the resurrection to win this battle. The power that raised Jesus from the dead is greater than all the combined physical forces of the universe. That is the same power that saves the sinner, raises the dead in the coming rapture of God's people and becomes the empowerment of the believer for victory in the battle with the world, the flesh and the devil.[1]

—Keith M. Bailey

Positional Thinker's Action #1

"I use the authority, delegated to me by Christ, which is as powerful as the power that raised Jesus from the dead and seated Him at God's right hand in the heavenly realms. This action defeated Satan, his demons, the world and my sinful nature. Christ gives me the authority over all of them."

The hope for the believer in tough circumstances is spiritual authority made possible by God when He raised Christ from the dead and seated Him at His right hand in the heavenly realms. Just before His ascension Jesus said, "All authority in heaven and on earth has been given to me" (Matthew 28:18). According to Hebrews 8:1 His authority was demonstrated when He "sat down at the right hand of the throne of the Majesty in heaven." The throne of God is the center of power of the whole universe. This power is committed to the ascended Lord Jesus Christ. Thus, the source of authority is God who raised Jesus from the dead through "the working of his mighty strength" (Ephesians 1:19). The working of God's mighty strength in raising Jesus from the dead is available to us because of our position in Christ. "And God raised us up with Christ and seated us with him in the heavenly realms in Christ Jesus" (2:6).

When I attended Nyack College I went with one of the students to the home of Dr. John A. MacMillan. My friend and other students were taking turns helping Dr. MacMillan just before his death. Meeting him personally motivated me to read his book, *The Authority of the Believer*, which has been invaluable in my ministry. This chapter contains highlights of what I have learned from him and other authors. Let me share the following experience of Dave, who was in bondage to the world, his sinful nature and the devil, and how he was delivered from his bondage by the authority of the believer.

From Swimming the Lake of Fire to Walking the Streets of Gold

Dave began attending our church. His mother drove him to church and picked him up later. He was unkempt and his body odor was offensive. I visited his home located in the neighborhood. He was quite intelligent and could quote verses from the Bible. He had attended church, but Vietnam changed his life. He explained that he had killed a lot of Viet Cong and was involved in booze, drugs and women. He also studied Buddhism. His wife was also an alcoholic.

When his tour of duty ended he flew home. Instead of being greeted with a hero's welcome he was greeted with loud jeers and was spit upon. He and his wife began attending AA meetings. She fell in love with one of the attendees and left Dave. He was devastated and one evening took a loaded revolver to his temple. He pulled the trigger and the bullet lodged in his brain. He was rushed to the hospital. The surgeons operated but had to leave the bullet in his brain or he would die.

Another elder and I visited him and would witness to him and pray for him but to no avail. At the conclusion of several visits after having a Bible study with him, he would boast, "One day I'm going to swim in the lake of fire."

He was on medication and was admitted periodically to the psychiatric ward of the V.A. Hospital. After a period of time I visited him at the hospital and shared with him with an open Bible the story of David's sins of committing adultery with Bathsheba and having her husband murdered. Then I related how David repented and read Psalm 51. I showed Dave where God said that

David was a man after His own heart. If David was forgiven for all of his sins and ended up being a man after God's own heart, cannot God forgive you? Dave agreed. The Holy Spirit finally got through to Dave.

"Why don't you pray and ask God to forgive you, to bring deliverance from your sinful habits and ask Jesus to come into your heart?" Dave prayed with a repentant spirit. He asked for forgiveness and asked Jesus to come into his heart. I prayed for Dave. I claimed my authoritative position over Satan and his forces of evil. I commanded Satan in the name of Jesus Christ to release Dave from bondage and to flee from him.

After I prayed, Dave shared his newfound joy of salvation and deliverance. He said, "I'm not going to swim in the lake of fire, but I'm going to walk the streets of gold."

Authority for Us Who Believe

The phrase "for us who believe" is the key that unlocks the power of God in the life of the Christian. We must understand that we have no power in ourselves, but we have authority which has been delegated to us.

Look at a president, senator, governor or policeman. Each one has something in common. He is vested with authority by the agency whom he serves. The power behind the president resides in the people who voted him into office. By his pen he can sign a bill that will affect the lives of everyone. The same is true of the senator or governor. The policeman also has authority delegated to him by his local community. He stands in the center of a busy intersection. Cars are whizzing by him. He blows his whistle and raises his hand. Suddenly the traffic stops. He signals the pedestrians to cross the street. What is the explanation? He is vested with the authority of the local government. Both the drivers and the pedestrians recognize the authority of his blue uniform and badge and obey him. When we are conscious of the divine power of God within us and of our own authority, we can face Satan and his demonic forces without fear or hesitation. K. Neill Foster writes of the authority of the believer, "The game's over for Satan. Jesus Christ, through the power of His death and resurrection, asserted and now maintains this position of authority. For Satan, it is already 'game over.' Now the delightful, awesome, even staggering truth is that the Christian believer, by virtue of his position in Jesus Christ, shares the Savior's total dominance over Satan."[2] As sharers of the Savior's total domination over Satan, let us exercise our authority as believers in all of our tough circumstances and illnesses.

Satan Rules from the Heavenlies

While the game's over for Satan as far as the Christian is concerned, he still rules the kingdoms of this world. He is called the "prince of this world" three times by Jesus in the book of John (12:31; 14:30; 16:11). Also, he "has blinded the minds of unbelievers" (2 Corinthians 4:4). All natural men are a part of the great world system that has dominated fallen humanity since the fall in the garden.

The seat of authority of Satan and his rebellious demonic rulers is located in the heavenly realms. Paul, in Ephesians 6:12, declares that we are fighting a spiritual war "against the powers of this dark world and against the spiritual forces of evil in the heavenly realms." While many believers recognize the reality of spiritual warfare, they don't realize it is being waged in the heavenly realms, and this is where the believer must do battle. Dr. Ed Murphy gives this insight in *The Handbook for Spiritual Warfare*:

> Here is Christ exalted in the heavenlies. Here is also the believer exalted with Him in the heavenlies. Here also are demonic powers warring against Christ and His church in the same heavenlies. Here is the church on earth and in the heavenlies declaring the wisdom of God to the principalities and powers in the heavenlies. This is high level, cosmic, spiritual warfare.[3]

"The heavenlies" is the place of the most intense conflict. Dr. MacMillan writes of the intense conflict of the believer who is aware of the high level, cosmic, spiritual warfare:

> He quickly realizes that he is a marked man. Whereas in his previous ministry, he may have firmly believed in the presence and working of the powers of darkness, and often earnestly prayed against them, there comes now a new consciousness of their existence and imminence. Bitterly they resent and resist his entrance into their domain, and his interference with their workings. Implacable and malignant, they concentrate their hatred against him in an intense warfare, in which there is no discharge.[4]

Where can we combat this intense warfare and these assaults successfully? The answer is that we are to sit on the throne level which is at the highest level, far above all of the evil powers of the heavenlies. Let us look at the throne level.

Sit on the Throne Level above Satan's Attacks

The highest heavenly realm level in the whole universe is God's throne level. Jesus is seated at the right hand of the throne and we by faith are also seated with Jesus. It is far above the enemy. If we remain by faith in this celestial location we are safe and secure in the Lord's headquarters of the universe.

Remember the Gulf War when the U.S. had the military advantage over Iraq with its superior air power? The U.S. was free in the heavens to unleash the tremendous fire power of bombs and smart missiles on the enemy below. The U.S. position above was powerful. When Iraq's planes did rise to the heavens to engage American planes, they were shot down.

We can visualize positional thinking in much the same way. Imagine a powerful military headquarters strategically located high in the mountains. Its position gives it a great military advantage over the enemy. But there are problems. An enemy stronghold lies in the valley below and we are held as the enemy's prisoner. There is no way to escape. Various forms of torture are used to break us down mentally, emotionally and physically.

Finally, one morning at dawn, friendly forces sweep down upon the prison in helicopters. In a daring rescue effort we and other captives are rescued and taken to the military headquarters in the mountains. Now our position has changed radically. We have been raised from a position of weakness, hopelessness and helplessness in the valley below to a position of strength and power on the mountaintop.

Was there anything we did in the rescue? Yes! By faith we cooperated fully in that rescue operation. Doesn't this picture remind us of our spiritual deliverance from the bondage of sin? Jesus came down from heaven to rescue us. In His rescue operation He raised us to the heavenly position and gave us the authority of the believer. In this position all the power of God comes from His throne to enable us to overcome Satan and our sinful nature. Whenever satanic forces, who have access to the heavenly realms, try to inflict damage, we can defeat them from the mountaintop level.

God has placed the Christian in a position of tremendous power. Positional power brings authority to the believer. When Christ defeated Satan He gave us redemption and victory over Satan and his demons. This spiritual power is based on our position in Christ. Our positional thinking comes from our position in Christ. We need to be aware of what our position in Christ means in warfare and appropriate our position by faith.

How did you begin your Christian life? It was not depending on your own doing, but upon what Christ did. By God's grace He has done everything for us in Christ. The Christian life is utter dependence upon the Lord Jesus. There is no limit to His grace. He freely bestows upon us His grace as we rest in Him.

Finally, the goal of the Christian life is the glory of God. There is no room for the glory of humanity in the work of God. God is jealous for His glory. Thus, everything begins and continues with His grace and its end design is the glory of God. Everything is to be to the praise of the glory of His grace (Ephesians 1:6, 12, 14).

Two

How Positional Thinking Differs from Positive Thinking

Therefore, since we have been justified through faith, we have peace with God through our Lord Jesus Christ. (Romans 5:1)

But thanks be to God! He gives us the victory through our Lord Jesus Christ. (1 Corinthians 15:57)

Justification is that act of God's grace whereby He declares righteous the person who places faith in Jesus Christ as his Substitute and Savior.[1]

—Harold M. Freligh

Positional Thinker's Action #2

"I rest in the victory already won by Jesus on the cross. By this act of God's grace I am justified, declared righteous and have eternal life and peace with God."

Relationship of Thinking and Faith

Some people may question the use of the phrase "positional thinking." They reason that "positional thinking" is not enough. Just thinking "position" doesn't mean that one will act on his position. They would prefer to use the phrase "positional believing," which implies faith.

According to Webster, a thinker is "a person who thinks in a specific way." The positional thinker sets his thinking on Jesus, who has broken the power of both Satan and our old sinful nature and has raised us to an authoritative position in the heavenly realms. Faith acts on this specific way of thinking, which is the reason I have presented thirteen actions of the positional thinker in this book. We need faith that "comes from hearing the message, and the message is heard through the word of Christ" (Romans 10:17). The essential idea of faith is faithfulness, devotion and steadfastness. Thus, the positional thinker's action includes faithfulness and steadfastness to the astounding, breathtaking truth that we rest in the victory over the devil already won by Jesus on the cross!

The Priority of Our Thought Life

Norman Wright believes our thought life identifies who we are, according to Proverbs 23:7: "For as he thinks in his heart, so is he" (NKJV). Wright observes the priority of the thought life in relation to the emotions: "Our thought life is both basic and important. God created us so that our feelings *follow* our thoughts. Many people today, however, have reversed the process and in so doing have a life of instability."[2]

Christian psychologists have also discovered a basic truth that is of tremendous help in understanding the place of emotions in relation to our thoughts: "The first thing to learn about analyzing our emotions is that we cannot control them directly. The reason is that they are side effects of something else that we can directly command, namely our thoughts."[3]

This being true, it then becomes important for us to learn how to put these facts to practical use. Here is how. Whenever a destructive emotion such as depression tries to take control of our hearts, we must think of the victory already won for us by Jesus. This is practicing the power of positional thinking. Instead of responding to these destructive emotions as we did when we lived under the control of our sinful natures, we now respond in a positive way based on Christ's victory on our behalf and our new position with Him. Satan knows the prime importance of the mind and has been battling for the control of our thoughts since the Garden of Eden. He first attacked the mind of Eve with deceit, according to Second Corinthians 11:3: "But I am afraid that just as Eve was deceived by the serpent's cunning, your minds may somehow be led astray from your sincere and pure devotion to Christ."

Our Position: Victory Already Won

However, there is hope, for Christ has taken His position of authority in the heavenly realms. "And having disarmed the powers and authorities, he made a public spectacle of them, triumphing over them by the cross" (Colossians 2:15). He has defeated Satan and all his forces of evil. We rest in that victory already won and given to us. Jesus warred against Satan and won. Through the cross He carried that warfare to the very threshold of hell itself. By the resurrection, God proclaimed His Son the victor over the whole realm of darkness, and this victory is extended to us. In Christ "we are more than conquerors through him who loved us" (Romans 8:37). Thus, we do not fight for victory, we fight *from* victory. We do not fight in order to win, for in Christ we have already won.

No believer can hope to enter the warfare of the ages without learning to rest in Christ and His finished work on the cross. The power of the Holy Spirit within us assists us in living practical, holy lives here on earth. When Satan attacks us through the thought life, he often uses a tough circumstance. Our first thought is to prepare for a big battle. This disturbs our rest in Christ and we pray, "Lord, please give me the victory." This is the starting point of our defeat. Why? Because we are asking God for something He has already given us.

This is what we should do when Satan attacks. First of all, be honest. Then pray, "Lord, I'm facing a situation that is difficult. The devil is trying to defeat me. I praise You that I already have Your victory!"

Don't try to work for a victory that you already have. Don't ask God to enable you to overcome the enemy. Just praise God because Jesus is the victor. Roy C. Putnam writes in his book, *In It to Win It*, the following words:

> He [Christ] is saying, "I want to enter your life so that together we may reign over every life situation." In every stormy, complex, erratic life situation He allows us to share in His triumph. . . . Every storm becomes an opportunity for Jesus to rise in our little human vessel and spread His peace. And ultimately we come to the place where we marvel, saying, "Lord, even the devils are subject to us through your name!"[4]

The power of positional thinking is the biblically healthy way of facing tough circumstances as a believer. Let us look at the differences between positive thinking and positional thinking in the following chart:

Differences between Positive Thinking and Positional Thinking

Positive Thinking (based on the old nature)	**Positional Thinking** (based on the new nature)
Self-centered	Christ-centered
Personal will power	Christ's resurrection power
Earthly	Heavenly
Humanistic	Biblical
Dead to God	Alive to God
Self-glorifying	God-glorifying
Goal: self-realization	Goal: to know Christ[5]

This book deals mainly with believers who are coping with chronic illnesses or life-threatening diseases. As we cope with our illness, God wants us to rest in the victory already won by His Son. Satan, however, tries to replace victory with discouraging defeat.

Our Position Rests on Justification

Justification could never have been conceived by the mind of man. We are not only forgiven when we are born again, but also are treated by God as though we have never sinned! This is only because Christ perfectly met the standard that God's law demands. He died in our place. Now He can justify the man who trusts Christ. Justification is an act of grace based on the finished work of Jesus. The person declared righteous is thereby free from guilt and punishment. Both justification and regeneration take place simultaneously. At the same time that God by His Spirit regenerates us, He who justifies treats us as though we had never sinned. Oh, the wonder of salvation through our Lord Jesus Christ!

The righteousness that God gives us is an imputed righteousness that can be illustrated by this incident. A traveler was driving through Switzerland when his new Rolls Royce broke down. When he phoned the dealer, the factory immediately sent out a mechanic with the necessary parts to fix the car. When the businessman later inquired about the bill for this expensive service call, the factory answered: "There is no record of any Rolls Royce breaking down."

In the same way, a Christian's sins are covered by Christ's cross. No record of the believer's sin exists in any of heaven's books. The believer is clothed in the imputed righteousness of Christ. "The blood of Jesus, [God's] Son, purifies us from all sin" (1 John 1:7).

Major Difference between Positive and Positional Thinking

Positive thinking is based on works while positional thinking is based on justification which is an act of God's grace. Positive thinkers are constantly striving to receive the victory over life's tough circumstances. The positional thinker rests in the victory already won by Jesus on the cross. Believers who are not aware of their victory position in Christ can be caught in a struggle to improve their condition in order to feel acceptable to God. But the believer who abides in the Lord Jesus, who takes Him as his righteousness and acceptance, is freed from this futile self-effort.

Since justification is in Christ and not in ourselves, it is a truth of position and not condition. We receive our justification in the Lord Jesus by faith in the Word. As we rest in our justified position, our spiritual condition is affected. We experience newfound peace, an increased joy of the Lord and a deeper sense of His love for us.

The Four Benefits of Justification

There are at least four spiritual benefits we derive from justification.

1. We are saved from wrath through Jesus. "Since we have now been justified by his blood, how much more shall we be saved from God's wrath through him!" (Romans 5:9).

2. Our sin question is settled.

 David says the same thing when he speaks of the blessedness of the man to whom God credits righteousness apart from works: "Blessed are they whose transgressions are forgiven, whose sins are covered. Blessed is the man whose sin the Lord will never count against him." (4:6-8)

3. We have peace with God. "Therefore, since we have been justified through faith, we have peace with God through our Lord Jesus Christ" (5:1).
4. We are made joint-heirs with Christ. "[S]o that, having been justified by his grace, we might become heirs having the hope of eternal life" (Titus 3:7). "Now if we are children, then we are heirs—heirs of God and co-heirs with Christ, if indeed we share in his sufferings in order that we may also share in his glory" (Romans 8:17).

These four benefits ought to motivate us to live for Him. They come packaged together in the gift of justification that Christ has given to all who have received Him as their personal Savior. If you are interested in receiving this free gift of God and these marvelous benefits, please read the closing paragraphs prayerfully.

The ABCs to Receive Justification and Eternal Life

A -Accept the Bible's diagnosis. The basic problem of humanity is a sin problem."For all have sinned and fall short of the glory of God" (3:23).

B -Believe Jesus died and was raised from the dead to heal your heart from sin. "Christ died for our sins according to the Scriptures, that he was buried, that he was raised on the third day" (1 Corinthians 15:3-4).

C -Confess your sins to Jesus. Confess "He is Lord." Receive spiritual healing and eternal life. "If we confess our sins, he is faithful and just and will forgive us our sins" (1 John 1:9). "That if you confess with your mouth, 'Jesus is Lord,' and believe in your heart that God raised him from the dead, you will be saved" (Romans 10:9).

Jesus comes into the heart of the person who has chosen God's ABCs to receive spiritual healing.

Sign the Consent Form Today!

If you have not received Christ Jesus into your life but agree with the ABCs of spiritual healing, receive Christ without delay. Pray this simple prayer:

> Dear Lord Jesus,
>
> I accept the Bible's diagnosis that I am a sinner. I thank You for dying on the cross to save me from my sins. I now repent of my sins. I confess that You are my Lord and believe in my heart that God raised You from the dead. I now receive You into my heart.
>
> In Jesus' name, Amen.

If you meant this prayer with all your heart, please sign this consent form. This simply says that you are in agreement with the Bible's diagnosis, that you need spiritual healing and are now submitting yourself to Jesus, the Great Physician. From this day forward, you will begin to rest in the victory won by Jesus on the cross.

Rx Consent Form

I hereby permit Jesus, the Great Physician, to:

1. Cleanse and heal my heart from all sin.
2. Dwell within my heart as my Savior and Lord.
3. Grant me the wonderful gift of spiritual life.

Name

____

Date ____________________

I have God's assurance that I have spiritual life according to God's Word. I have Jesus in my heart and have become the dwelling place of God. Now I have the power of God to cope with my tough circumstances or illness.

> This is the testimony: God has given us eternal life, and this life is in his Son. He who has the Son has life; he who does not have the Son of God does not have life.
>
> I write these things to you who believe in the name of the Son of God so that you may know that you have eternal life. (1 John 5:11-13)

THREE

Think Co-Crucifixion

I have been crucified with Christ and I no longer live, but Christ lives in me. The life I live in the body, I live by faith in the Son of God, who loved me and gave himself for me. (Galatians 2:20)

"My sinful self, thou hateful thing, breaking out now in pride, and now in passion, and now in jealousy, and now in indolence, and now in selfishness, breaking out in a thousand hateful forms; my sinful self, I put thee where the sinless Christ put thee, on the cross."[1]

—J. Gregory Mantle

Positional Thinker's Action #3

"I believe that co-crucifixion is my 'death position' with Christ's death, which has broken the power of the sinful nature over me."

We need to center our thinking on Christ's crucifixion, resurrection and ascension that have made our positional thinking possible. These three events, which are the crux of Easter, are also the basis of defeating Satan and delivering the believer from the bondage of sin. The victorious Christian experience follows the Easter pattern. Christ's death and burial came first on Good Friday. Second, His resurrection occurred on Easter Sunday. Third, forty days later, Jesus ascended to His Father's throne in heaven. Jesus, through His death, has broken the power of the old sinful nature in those of us who believe. By His crucifixion, resurrection and ascension He has raised us to an authoritative position in the heavenly realm.

The Easter model was God's way to develop holiness in the believer. The Word says in Hebrews 12:14, "Make every effort to live in peace with all men and to be holy; without holiness no one will see the Lord." Since the Word tells us to make every effort to be holy, we need to discover how the believer develops in holiness.

In the last chapter we saw that it is by God's grace that true believers have been justified by faith through the finished work of Christ on the cross. Believers need to rest in this victory won by Jesus. Because of Calvary, we are declared righteous, we receive God's gift of eternal life and our hearts are at peace with Him.

Picture a large chalkboard covering a wall of a huge room. On the board are listed all of your sins and the dates they were committed. I would imagine my sins would be in tiny print in order to fit them on the board because there are so many. According to the marvelous doctrine of justification by Christ's death on the cross, He wiped the slate clean through His blood. Not only did He erase our sin record, but He also treats us, in Christ, just as though we had never sinned. This means we all begin on an equal basis with a clean slate. However, the big problem is trying to keep the slate clean from new sins.

The answer is sanctification. We will look at positional and experiential sanctification in relationship to co-crucifixion and the crisis experience. We will see that it is the call of the Christian to become in experience what he already has in his positional sanctification. It is also essential to understand the traits of the sinful nature and how it effects the believer, especially during tough circumstances. This is the main theme of this book.

In the way of review and emphasis, there are two lifestyles to cope with adversity . The first is positive thinking which is based on the old nature and draws its energy from it. The other is positional thinking which draws its energy from the Holy Spirit. It should be clear that this book is based not on positive, but *positional* thinking.

The Battle within the Believer

After conversion the believer aspires to please the Lord. However, he experiences a battle within himself. The Bible teaches that the old sinful nature and the new spiritual nature are at war within the believer. The old nature can do nothing but sin. It cannot know, obey nor please God (Romans 8:7). It cannot be improved, since it is unchangeable and remains in the believer as long as he lives on earth.

But every believer has a new nature that cannot sin. By contrast, it knows, obeys and pleases God. These two natures coexist in every believer and make his inner life a battle. Look at the apostle Paul. A conflict waged between the old Saul and the new Paul. Romans 7 describes the conflict raging within: "For what I want to do I do not do, but what I hate I do. . . . I know that nothing good lives in me, that is, in my sinful nature. For I have the desire to do what is good, but I cannot carry it out" (7:15, 18).

This same conflict staggers many young believers. They find themselves doing the old things again. The sinful habits return; the joy of fellowship with Christ lessens. Discouragement follows. They struggle against their sins and pray for release, but to no avail. One day, in despair, they cry out, "What a wretched man I am! Who will rescue me from this body of death?" (7:24). Has this been your experience?

Generally, through growth in the Word, the believer sees by the illumination of the Holy Spirit that the battle within him is between the old and new natures. He sees that he will never be rid of the old self-life and that no good thing can come out of it. The best things that he is capable of doing, such as good works, along with the worst things that he is capable of doing, can't sanctify him. He could feed the poor, tithe to his local church and raise money to build a hospital, but it would do no good. God's answer to the self-life is crucifixion! The young believer, after going through the Romans 7 struggle sees that the answer is in Romans 8. Instead of the "I" (his own sinful nature), he sees the mention of the

Spirit in the first sixteen verses of Romans 8. Instead of being controlled by the sinful nature he submits himself in full surrender to the control of the Spirit of Christ (8:9). In this crisis experience he identifies himself as being co-crucified with Christ.

In the final analysis, sanctification is a person—Jesus Christ! "It is because of him that you are in Christ Jesus, who has become for us wisdom from God—that is, our righteousness, holiness and redemption" (1 Corinthians 1:30).

Sanctification Is Both Positional and Experiential

Positional sanctification takes place at salvation. "And by that will, we have been made holy through the sacrifice of the body of Jesus Christ once for all" (Hebrews 10:10). Those who are sanctified are those who are saved through the merits of Christ. In Second Thessalonians 2:13, Paul told the Thessalonians, "[F]rom the beginning God chose you to be saved through the sanctifying work of the Spirit and through belief in the truth." The Holy Spirit set believers apart in Christ's death once for all. This was a perfect work that never needs to be repeated. *Positionally* we are spiritually perfect in Christ. But our *experiential* sanctification will never be fully perfected until we reach heaven. We will attain our sinless perfection when we see Christ and shall be like Him (1 John 3:2).

Entering into co-crucifixion is a crisis experience—can you think of any greater crisis than dying on a cross? It leads one into a closer walk with God, to a place of full surrender where Jesus is all to us. However, this cannot happen until He has *all* of us. This full surrender takes us into experiential sanctification which is walking in the Spirit, and the evidence is the fruit of the Spirit.

The teachings of this book are closely tied to sanctification, for sanctification and positional thinking go together. God uses the avenue of tough circumstances to develop Christlike holiness of life in us, along with a ministry that touches others with the gospel. Sanctification is that work of grace whereby the believer is separated from self and inward sinfulness, and by the filling of the Holy Spirit, is set apart for holiness and service. This is both a crisis and a progressive experience wrought in the life of the believer subsequent to conversion. Hebrews 9:14 connects the work of the Holy Spirit to Christ's crucifixion. "How much more, then, will the blood of Christ, who through the eternal Spirit offered himself unblemished to God, cleanse our consciences from acts that lead to death, so that we may serve the living God!"

The Holy Spirit strengthened Jesus to offer Himself as the pure, spotless sacrificial Lamb of God to die for us. The eternal Spirit ministered to Christ as He hung upon the cross, enabling Him to complete His mission of death and resurrection that we might have life. As the Holy Spirit enabled Christ to die, so He enables us to die to our old sinful nature.

We must cooperate with the Holy Spirit in keeping the "old man" crucified through a process of "count[ing ourselves] dead to sin but alive to God in Christ Jesus" (Romans 6:11). Through the crucifixion of the old man with Christ, the believer has been made dead to sin. Through grace, the old man was nailed to the cross and buried in the tomb; through faith, the old man will be kept there. Continuously count yourself to be totally dead from all that belongs to the old life.

> Therefore do not let sin reign in your mortal body so that you obey its evil desires. Do not offer the parts of your body to sin, as instruments of wickedness, but rather offer yourselves to God, as those who have been brought from death to life; and offer the parts of your body to him as instruments of righteousness. (6:12-13)

The call for the Christian is to become in experience what he already is in position—dead to sin (6:5-7) and alive to God (6:8-10). The second step toward the Christian's victory over sin is a refusal to let sin reign in his life (6:12). The third step is to offer himself to God (6:13).

Old Sinful Nature Is Satan's Stamp upon Humanity

Satan's connection to us is through our old sinful nature with which we were born into this world. We were all born as self-centered beings with the tendency to sin, to break the Law and to live for the world system, which is under the domination of the prince of this world. Our need is to move from identification with Satan as soon as possible to identification with Christ in His death.

The following Scriptures show four aspects of our identification with Christ in His death:

1. *Death to Self.* "[H]e died . . . that those who live should no longer live for themselves but for him" (2 Corinthians 5:15).
2. *Death to Sin.* "We died to sin; how can we live in it any longer?" (Romans 6:2).

3. *Death to the Law.* "[B]y dying to what once bound us, we have been released from the law so that we serve in the new way of the Spirit" (7:6).
4. *Death to the World.* "Since you died with Christ to the basic principles of this world, why, as though you still belonged to it, do you submit to its rules?" (Colossians 2:20).

Illustration of Being Dead and Buried with Christ

In the fourth century in Egypt a young brother sought out the great Macarius. "Father," he said, "what is the meaning of being dead and buried with Christ?"

"My son," answered Macarius, "do you remember our dear brother who died, and was buried a short time ago? Go now to his grave, and tell him all the unkind things that you ever heard of him, and that we are glad he is dead, and thankful to be rid of him, for he was such a worry to us, and caused so much discomfort in the church. Go, my son, and say that and hear what he will answer."

The young man was surprised and doubted whether he really understood, but Macarius only said, "Do as I bid you, my son, and come and tell me what our departed brother says."

The young man did as he was commanded, and returned.

"Well, and what did our brother say?" asked Macarius.

The young brother exclaimed, "How could he say anything? He is dead."

"Go now again, my son, and repeat every kind and flattering thing you have ever heard of him; tell him how much we miss him; how great a saint he was; what noble work he did; how the whole church depended upon him; and come again and tell me what he says."

The young man began to see the lesson Macarius would teach him. He went again to the grave and addressed many flattering comments to the dead man, and then returned to Macarius. "He answers nothing, father; he is dead and buried."

"You know now, my son," said the old father, "what it is to be dead with Christ. Praise and blame equally are nothing to him who is really dead and buried with Christ."

As you become identified with the crucifixion of Christ and rest in the victory given to you over the world, the sinful nature and Satan, think of these blessed shifts in sanctification:

Think of These Important Shifts in Sanctification

Before you were concerned about being happy,
But now being more like Jesus.
Before you lived and worked for Christ,
But now you let Him work through you.
Before you were interested in yourself,
But now in who you are in Christ Jesus.
Before you were in the condition of weakness,
But now in the position of strength.
Before it was "I,"
But now it is "Christ!"

Our thinking of the "old I" in Galatians 2:20 has radically changed. This shift in our thinking can be placed in the following way: "I [the old I] am crucified with Christ: nevertheless I [the new I] live; yet not I [the old I], but Christ liveth in me: and the life which I [I plus Christ] now live in the flesh I [I plus Christ] live by the faith [His faith] of the Son of God, who loved me, and gave himself for me" (KJV).

We must ever keep the holiness of God in our thoughts. Holiness describes both the majesty of God and the purity and moral perfection of His nature. Positional and experiential sanctification is His method of developing holiness within us. Positional thinking rests on His holiness for the preservation and moral health of humanity. Whoever is holy is spiritually healthy. Anyone who is contrary to holiness will fall under the wrath of God along with Satan, his army, the sinful nature and the present world system of evil. Holiness protects the saints for their eternal, holy home in heaven!

Are you discouraged because you have been battling with sin in your life? You have prayed for release, but to no avail. You have been experiencing the struggle within your heart between the old and new natures and are crying out, "What a wretched man I am!" After reading this chapter, has the Holy Spirit shown you that Jesus Christ not only died to save you from your sins but also to save you from yourself? Will you say, "I believe that co-crucifixion is my 'death position' with Christ's death which has broken the power of my sinful nature over me"? Then pray in repentance and by faith accept the death and burial of your sinful nature along with Christ's death and burial. Then from your death position accept your risen life position with Christ. The next chapter will deal with this exciting truth!

FOUR

Think Co-Resurrection

And God raised us up with Christ and seated us with him in the heavenly realms in Christ Jesus. (Ephesians 2:6)

By His mighty power God raised Christ from the dead. But the miracle of that resurrection was not that Christ came forth Himself. I would have accepted that. . . . But the miracle of the resurrection is this: when Christ came forth He brought a new humanity with Him.[1]

—Roy C. Putnam

Positional Thinker's Action #4

"I believe that co-resurrection is my 'risen life position' with Christ's resurrection, and I claim His resurrection power for strength through suffering and healing for my spirit, soul and body."

When you read the words of Ephesians 2:6, "*And God raised us up*" (emphasis added), think co-resurrection! In the Easter model the grave could not hold Christ; He was raised from the dead. We are identified with Christ in His resurrection. Our new nature is alive. Thus, when a negative emotion such as depression or fear tries to gain control, we must not only think the "death position" to the old nature, but also the "risen life position" of the new nature. This positional truth has strengthened me when coping with the spiritual, social and psychological damages of cancer.

Since my bout with cancer, I begin my day with prayer saying, "Lord Jesus, thank You for Your death and resurrection for me. I count my old self to be dead with Your death and my new self to be alive through Your resurrection. As I take my seat with You in the heavenlies, I claim Your resurrection power for this day." This has helped me for years to experience resurrection power over tough circumstances.

We need to see that the Holy Spirit enables us to have resurrection life. "And if the Spirit of him who raised Jesus from the dead is living in you, he who raised Christ from the dead will also give life to your mortal bodies through his Spirit, who lives in you" (Romans 8:11). This passage connects the resurrection of Jesus with the work of the Holy Spirit. The Holy Spirit gives life to our mortal bodies, which are subject to death. It is the Spirit who dwells within who *quickens* us. This word literally means "the exhilarating and reviving of a waning and exhausted person." This divine quickening of our mortal body is one of the privileges of our life in the Spirit.

Co-Resurrection Follows Co-Crucifixion

> The death he died, he died to sin once for all; but the life he lives, he lives to God.
>
> In the same way, count yourselves dead to sin but alive to God in Christ Jesus. (6:10-11)

"Count" is a bookkeeper's word. Here it means the ledger shows that in my position with Christ I died to this evil, sinful nature within me when He died on the cross. Dr. A.B. Simpson said of co-crucifixion, " 'I have been crucified with Christ,' not my sins, or my sinful nature, but 'I' the old man, the former individual. Both good and bad have died alike, my strength and my weakness, my sin and my self-sufficiency, my good qualities and my bad, and henceforth it is no more I, but Christ that liveth in me . . ." He warns us: "We must not be everlastingly getting crucified over again . . . but we must count it once for all done and finished and we must steadily reckon that it is so."[2]

Co-Resurrection Makes It Possible to Live a New Life

> By no means! We died to sin; how can we live in it any longer? . . . We were therefore buried with him through baptism into death in order that, just as Christ was raised from the dead through the glory of the Father, we too may live a new life. (6:2, 4)

Baptism demonstrates that we died with Christ in order to live a new life with Christ. It was Christ who was raised from the dead through the glory of the Father, showing at once the believer's union with Christ. When Paul answered his critics with the words, "We died to sin; how can we live in it any longer?" (6:2), he was declaring to the world that their lifestyle need no longer be controlled by sin, which implies that Satan was no longer their master. Don J. Kenyon, in his interpretation of Romans, writes the following:

> It is as though Paul were saying in effect that this great conflict between darkness and light, God and Satan, Christ and Adam, truth and wrath, is now settled once for all. The victory is to be found in grace through Christ's death and resurrection.[3]

God has given to us, in our daily spiritual warfare, victory over sin, self, Satan and the world system. When we are placed in Him in His death and burial, we are raised with Christ from the dead that we may live a new kind of life. This new kind of life is to walk daily and hourly in the resurrection life. This is what Paul meant when he proclaimed, "I have been crucified with Christ and I no longer live, but Christ lives in me. The life [that risen life] I live in the body, I live by faith in the Son of God, who loved me and gave himself for me" (Galatians 2:20).

Co-Resurrection Produces the Fruit of Holiness

> . . . you also died to the law through the body of Christ, that you might belong to another, to him who was raised from the dead, in order that we might bear fruit to God. (Romans 7:4)

Holiness is the fruit of our union with Jesus made possible by His resurrection from the dead. If Jesus had not been resurrected, the Holy Spirit would not have come to reside in the believer. But the Comforter did come on the Day of Pentecost. His ministry produces the fruit of the Spirit in the life of the believer. "The fruit of the Spirit is love, joy, peace, patience, kindness, goodness, faithfulness, gentleness and self-control" (Galatians 5:22-23). Christ's criteria for Christian character is the fruit of the Spirit.

The Christian is called upon to become in daily experience what he is positionally in Christ in order to bear the fruit of the Spirit. Notice, first of all, the teaching of these phrases taken from Colossians 3:1-14. (It would be helpful to read this passage in its entirety from your Bible.) The position of the believer in Christ is described as follows:

1. He is dead (3:5).
2. He has been raised with Christ (3:1).
3. He is with Christ in heaven (3:3).
4. He has taken off the old self (3:9).
5. He has put on the new self (3:10).

The believer is instructed to practice his position (experiential sanctification):

1. He is to set his heart (or mind) on things above (3:1-2).
2. He is to put to death practices that belong to his earthly nature (3:5).
3. He is to rid himself of practices that characterize his unregenerate self (3:8).

The Christian has the responsibility to live a godly life, described as "clothing yourselves":

> Therefore, as God's chosen people, holy and dearly loved, clothe yourselves with compassion, kindness, humility, gentleness and patience. . . . And

> over all these virtues put on love, which binds them all together in perfect unity. (3:12, 14)

These verses are another example of the fruit of the Spirit, as this chapter is another example of the work of sanctification in the life of the believer. Since we have been made alive to God by the resurrection of Christ, we have the power of the Holy Spirit within us to help us live a new life.

Dr. George Pardington describes beautifully what the sanctified life is all about:

> [H]e is alive toward God. Indeed, the deep work of sanctification awakens and stirs up every spiritual sense. By the heavenly anointing our eyes are opened to see divine truth (Revelation 3:18) and our ears are opened to hear the "still small voice" or the "gentle whisper" of God (1 Kings 19:12). Our taste is renewed to feast on the "living bread" (John 6:51), and our feelings are refined to detect the loving touch of God (Mark 10:13). By the infilling of the Holy Spirit, then, our whole being is made "alive to God." Every faculty and power within the believer is awakened to a new order of vitality and energy.[4]

Co-Resurrection Confirms Satan's Defeat

One of my unforgettable experiences in basic training on maneuvers was stepping on the head of a copperhead snake. I was running with a group of soldiers on a narrow winding path in a thickly wooded and underbrush area. Suddenly a copperhead slithered in front of me and I stepped on its head with the heal of my boot. I jumped quickly out of the way yelling, "A snake, a snake, I've stepped on a snake!" While the stunned and bruised snake squirmed, the soldier behind me quickly took his trench shovel from his belt and struck the deathblow to the serpent.

We had been warned about the snake-infested area earlier. The advance group had cleared the area for our tents and killed a huge king snake in the process. They nailed it to a tree where it hung full length to greet us as we entered the campsite.

The Bible warns us from cover to cover of the spiritual warfare with the old serpent, the devil. The Lord prophesied of this warfare beginning with the fall in Eden and onward. Genesis 3:15 declares, "And I will put enmity between you and the woman, and between your offspring and hers; he will crush your head, and you will strike his heel." This is a promise of victory over Satan, sin and death. It is brought about by one who is declared to be the seed of the woman. Biologically, seed comes from the man, not the woman. When the Scripture says "her seed" meaning the seed of the woman, we are given a clue that a new and marvelous miracle is in the making—a virgin birth! Jesus was born of the virgin Mary.

With the words, "he [referring to Christ] will crush your head," Moses is declaring that Jesus would mortally wound Satan, leading to his ultimate judgment. The striking of the heel is fulfilled with the crucifixion of Christ, by whose stripes we are healed. Peter wrote, "He himself bore our sins in his body on the tree, so that we might die to sins and live for righteousness; by his wounds you have been healed" (1 Peter 2:24).

The Footprint of Jesus on the Back of the Serpent's Neck

In Old Testament times when a king was defeated, the conquering king forced the defeated one to lie facedown on the ground. Then in full view of the crowd, the victorious king placed his foot upon the neck of the conquered enemy showing total victory. Because of the resurrection of Jesus, Satan is a defeated foe. The way to handle adversity is to think co-resurrection and see Christ's foot upon the neck of the defeated old serpent. Jesus is Victor!

Roy Putnam records what one missionary says when trouble and threat come to him: he personifies it (the trouble and threat) and says, "Bend over. I want to see the back of your neck! Just as I thought! The footprint of the Son of God is upon it. Be gone!" Paul was saying the same thing when in Romans 16 he braced the early Christians by prophesying, "And the God of peace shall bruise Satan under your feet shortly" (16:20, KJV).[5]

Co-Resurrection Gives Victory over Suffering

The apostle Paul writes, "We know that the whole creation has been groaning as in the pains of childbirth right up to the present time. . . . We ourselves . . . groan inwardly as we wait eagerly for . . . the redemption of our bodies" (Romans 8:22-23). A big question often raised is, "How could a good and loving God create such a world of sin and suffering, even death?" John F. Walvoord offers this answer:

> The answer is that he did not; man's choosing the path of sin caused this. As illustrated in the curse pronounced on Adam and Eve, they would now labor in a difficult world of pain, suffering, sweat, toil and death. Our present world with its sickness, catastrophe, earthquakes, sorrow and death exemplifies the results of sin.[6]

Walvoord concludes with these words on the whole issue of human suffering:

> The disordered world is the result of sin, and only the order Christ himself can bring into the human life or to the world as a whole, as in the millennial kingdom, will restore peace and victory.[7]

Our co-resurrection takes us through suffering and develops Christlikeness in us. Don't have a pity party or waste your time complaining. Recognize that God is using your suffering to conform you into Christlike character. Exercise your authority!

A Parable of a Suffering Teacup

I heard a parable of a teacup sitting on a shelf. This teacup had a story to tell of its suffering. The teacup said, "I was just a gray ugly lump of clay. My master picked me up and began to shape me. I was pliable but his strong fingers hurt me. He placed me on a wheel which began to spin. I shouted, 'Stop. You are making me dizzy. I'm throwing up!'

"Next he placed me in an oven which soon became very hot. I complained, saying, 'Take me out of here. It's too hot!'

"When my master painted me, I shouted, 'The fumes from the paint are killing me. Furthermore, I don't like the design or the color.'

"The master rebuked me and made the oven twice as hot this time. I snarled saying, 'I can't take any more heat!' "

After a period of time the master took the cup out of the oven. He said to the cup, "Look into this mirror."

The teacup looked into the mirror and was taken by surprise at its image. The cup said with great humility and appreciation, "Forgive me for all of my complaining. Forgive me, master, for my impatience. You created and fashioned me from that formless piece of gray clay into a one-of-a-kind, beautifully shaped cup."

Can we not identify with the experience of that teacup? We must remember that our growth into Christlikeness often comes in the heat of the oven.

Job's Belief in the Future Resurrection Helped Him in Suffering

Job is the classic example of suffering because of the enmity of Satan. God permitted the hedge of protection to be lifted from Job, and Satan attacked him. The devil wastes no time in performing his wicked deeds. He uses human instruments to carry out his plans. The Sabians took Job's animals and killed his servants. The Chaldeans devastated his property. At this point, Satan began to use natural forces to complete the destruction. A fire broke out and a great wind collapsed the houses, killing Job's sons and daughters. Satan also caused painful, running sores to break out all over Job's body, from the top of his head to the bottom of his feet. While Job is scraping his painful sores with a broken piece of pottery, his wife asks, "Why are you still trusting in God? Why don't you curse God and die?" (Job 2:9, author paraphrase).

Satan had gotten to Job's wife. Thus, she spoke the very desire of the devil. Satan often uses a person who is the closest to you to defeat you. In this most difficult of painful circumstances, Job remained faithful and Satan was soundly defeated. McCandlish Phillips writes in his classic book, *The Spirit World*: "Yet Job did not sin with his lips. The end of it was complete vindication for God, complete vindication for Job, and complete defeat for Satan. Satan understood now that there was a man upon the earth who loved God *solely for Himself*."[8]

The ultimate vindication expressed by Job was his belief in his future resurrection. Setting his thinking on the resurrection position is the highlight of this book. Job shouted with a cry of victorious assurance: "I know that my Redeemer lives, and that in the end he will stand upon the earth" (Job 19:25).

As it helped Job, it helps us today. But even more so because the resurrection of Jesus has been accomplished. Co-resurrection has followed co-crucifixion. Christ was delivered over to death for our sins and was raised to life for our justification. The resurrection was God's seal of approval on Christ's death.

Think and practice your co-resurrection!
Enjoy your risen-life position of victory!

FIVE

Think Co-Seated

And God raised us up with Christ and seated us with him in the heavenly realms in Christ Jesus. (Ephesians 2:6)

Paul prays that the eyes of our heart may be enlightened (Ephesians 1:18) to understand all that is contained for us in this double fact, that God has first by mighty power "made him to sit with Him," and then by grace "made us to sit with Him." And the first lesson we must learn is this, that the work is not initially ours at all, but His. It is not that we work for God, but that He works for us. God gives us a position of rest. He brings His Son's finished work and presents it to us, and then He says to us, "Please sit."[1]

—Watchman Nee

Positional Thinker's Action #5

"I am co-seated with Christ in the heavenly realms, where I am assured of victory as I actively engage in spiritual warfare against the world, the sinful nature and the devil."

We have been following three orderly events in our positional experience that are patterned after the Easter model. Christ's crucifixion and burial came first; secondly, His resurrection on Easter Sunday; and forty days later His ascension. When we take our position of co-crucifixion and co-resurrection we also are co-seated with Christ in the heavenly realms. Thus, think co-seated. When you think of Ephesians 2:6, think of sitting together with Christ in heaven.

Christ not only died and arose, but He also ascended to the heavenly realms. The believer has been elevated with the ascended Christ to the celestial realms where he is made a partaker of Christ's throne. Christ's position is at the right hand of God, and ours is with Christ. Our co-seated position "with Him" is a dignified position. From it, Jesus has delegated to us the authority of the believer over satanic threats. The authority of the believer assures us of victory against the assaults of the world, the sinful nature and the devil. It is a right made available to every believer (see Ephesians 1:19-20).

God Is in Heaven on His Throne

I had just arrived at church and was seated alone at my desk. I heard someone outside the door. A young man in his mid-twenties entered the room. He had a red scarf hanging down over his head. He pulled off the scarf, exposing a completely shaved bald head. He introduced himself with a scowl on his face and boastfully said in a loud voice, "I am God!"

I countered his wild claim in an equally loud voice saying, "No, you are not. God is on His throne in heaven!" Then I asked, "How did you get into the church building because the doors are all locked?"

The young man said, "A voice spoke to me and told me to climb through a window."

"Show me the window where you came in."

He led me to the room where we kept the church records and years of offering envelopes. Boxes of offering envelopes were dumped and scattered all over the floor. I was stunned at the clutter!

At that moment I heard the outside door open and shut. Mrs. Marck had arrived to clean the church. "Just a minute," I said. "I'll be right back. The cleaning lady has arrived."

I rushed out of the room and quickly, yet quietly told Mrs. Marck about the break-in and the offering envelopes. "Would you please telephone the police?" I whispered.

"Yes," she replied.

I rushed back and began to witness to the young deluded man.

He said, "I'm religious. I celebrated communion upstairs."

When he mentioned communion, I recognized the red scarf as being the communion table covering.

He said, "Since it was cold in the chapel I fixed the furnace."

Oh, no. What else? I thought to myself.

Just then the police arrived and I filed a report. They took the young man to a psychiatric ward.

After they had gone, we went upstairs to the chapel. The communion elements weren't kept in the church. He had found some candy corn left over from a party and celebrated his communion by eating candy corn. When we checked the furnace room he had disassembled some parts for the furnace which were lying on the floor. He had also taken tubes from the organ.

We repaired the damage, but didn't press charges.

Like this person, Satan deceitfully tries to come into the life of the church through a back window. He causes destruction whenever and wherever he can. Arrogantly claiming to be God, he tries to frighten us. This pride was his original sin which caused his downfall along with a host of fallen angels. This started spiritual warfare before the earth was formed, a conflict that will continue until Satan, his demonic forces and his followers are cast into eternal hell!

Four Benefits We Receive from the Ascension

There are four benefits we receive from the ascension of Jesus.

1. We can be assured of a home in heaven because of the ascension. When Jesus ascended, He was transferred from earth to heaven. He had successfully completed His mission of redemption on earth. This sinful world is not a suitable home for our Redeemer in His state of exaltation. But one day it will undergo a great process of regeneration and become a new heaven and a new earth.

2. We have delegated authority because of the ascension. Jesus said, "All authority in heaven and on earth has been given to me" (Matthew 28:18). There are many examples of this authority in action. With His authority, He commissioned the disciples for their task of world evangelism and guaranteed them victory in spiritual warfare. In Luke10, Jesus delegated total authority over all the dimensions of evil supernaturalism to His twelve apostles, as well as to the seventy-two disciples (10:1, 17-19). Later, He established a team ministry when He sent them out two by two. Jesus showed the spiritual authority behind those in godly agreement when He said, "If two of you on earth agree about anything you ask for, it will be done for you by my Father in heaven. For where two or three come together in my name, there I am with them" (Matthew 18:19-20).
3. We can experience the filling of the Holy Spirit on account of the ascension. It was necessary that Christ return to the Father in order for the Holy Spirit to come upon all believers and fill them. "Unless I go away, the Counselor will not come to you; but if I go, I will send him to you" (John 16:7). This is the source of the power behind the authority of the believer.
4. We will participate with Christ in His return as a result of the ascension. Jesus needed to ascend to eventually come again with power and great glory to reign on earth. Theologian John F. Walvoord writes,

> The book of Revelation, as no other book in the Bible, provides a comprehensive picture of the glory of Christ, God's plan for his exaltation and victory over sin, and with it the revelation of the glorious future for the children of God. . . . Furthermore,

> the book describes God's ultimate purpose of revealing Jesus Christ, which is its central theme, and characterizes his second coming and his subsequent reign on earth as well as his position in the new heaven and the new earth.[2]

The Seat of Authority of Satan and Demons Is in the Heavenlies

We noted in chapter one that Satan rules from the heavenlies. His seat of authority along with his demonic armies is located in that realm. Our spiritual warfare is "against the powers of this dark world and against the spiritual forces of evil in the heavenly realms" (Ephesians 6:12). It is in this arena that we do our battle against our enemy.

These rebellious spiritual rulers have dominated the human race since its fall. What is their activity? Evil is the name of their game. Their strategy is deception. Innumerable wicked spirits stir up animal passions, hatred, strife and numberless acts of wickedness. They use tough circumstances such as illnesses to discourage people to give up and question God's love for them. They are present in seances, false prophecies and witchcraft, and control millions through astrology and cults.

Being Co-Seated with Christ Assures the Believer of Rest

The book of Ephesians tells us three important truths vital to the Christian life: 1) How to live in the heavenly realms while on earth, 2) How to walk on earth while living in the heavenly realms, and 3) How to rest in faith while fighting the foe.

The Christian is given power that enables him to rest from his own work and enter into the Sabbath rest. In the Old Testament people worked six days and then rested. The order of Ephesians, however, is for believers to rest and then work. We must first learn to practice the power of positional thinking which rests upon our co-seated position with Christ in the heavenly realms. This enables us to rest, but not from action. This is rest instead of stress. It is rest from friction and fretfulness.

Hebrews 4:3 gives us a marvelous insight into rest: "Now we who have believed enter that rest, just as God has said." The rest God calls us to enter (4:10-11) is not our rest, but His, which He invites us to share with Him. We rest in victory provided for us.

Stay Seated to Enjoy Security

Christians must recognize that the only safe place is to stay seated with Christ. If we remain faithful, our mountaintop fortress that is "far above" all the forces of evil will protect us.

I remember reading of a pilot in World War II who discovered a rat that was gnawing on a vital wire. This severed wire would cause his plane to go out of control and crash. Quickly he pulled back his joystick, increased his speed and soared upward into the atmosphere. With his oxygen mask secured he continued his ascent to where oxygen was scarce. In this rarefied atmosphere the rat soon died and the pilot was safe and secure from his destructive enemy. In a similar fashion, we are safe and secure as long as we stay seated in our heavenly position. The devil can't stand the rarefied atmosphere of heaven's love and holiness. However. if we succumb to the pressures and leave our seats, we are open to attack.

When I was a soldier, I knew I had responsibilities. I could not be passive if we were to win the war. Even though we might have had superior weapons, they weren't enough to win the war. If I decided to be passive and not wear my helmet or carry my weapons, and the enemy infiltrated, guess who would have been one of the first soldiers to be picked off?

As a soldier in the Lord's army, I have the assurance that God has provided in Christ a winning strategy. He also has designed effective weapons to secure victory over the forces of evil. But I know that if I don't do my part, I may end up a casualty.

Six

Test the Spirits

Dear friends, do not believe every spirit, but test the spirits to see whether they are from God, because many false prophets have gone out into the world. This is how you can recognize the Spirit of God: Every spirit that acknowledges that Jesus Christ has come in the flesh is from God, but every spirit that does not acknowledge Jesus is not from God. This is the spirit of the antichrist. (1 John 4:1-3)

Our psychiatrists know full well how long and tedious the treatment for a mentally deranged person can be. Possessed people, on the other hand, can be delivered almost instantaneously when they come into contact with the Lord Jesus Christ.[1]

—Kurt Koch

Positional Thinker's Action #6

"I renounce the spirit of error and rebuke every spirit that doesn't acknowledge that Jesus Christ has come in the flesh. I will seek the guidance of a godly person who has the spiritual gift of discernment to help with demonic cases."

The Bureau of Standards, located in Washington, DC, keeps the official weights and measures for the United States. An official yardstick and an official pound are protected in enclosures so that they remain precisely accurate all the time. The weights and measures of the United States have come from these originals.

The standard or measure of our Christian faith is the Word of God. Jesus is the Word (John 1:1) who became flesh and lived among us (1:14). The test rests on believing that Jesus, the Messiah, has come in the flesh as God-man to provide Salvation.

What do you think of Christ? The answer to this question determines truth and error. The Bible teaches that Jesus Christ, the carpenter of Galilee, is God. He is the creator of the universe. Thomas doubted until he saw the resurrected Jesus. Then he said, "My Lord and my God" (John 20:28).

Two warnings are declared. One, "Do not believe every spirit" (1 John 4:1). We must not believe everything we hear and fall for it hook, line and sinker. "Do not believe" is more correctly translated "stop believing" which implies that some Christians were already being carried away by the spirits of error. Two, "but test the spirits to see whether they are from God" (4:1). We need to pray that the Lord will help us to have a sanctified sense of judgment to recognize the spirits at work. The following method of testing the spirits comes from the Word of God and is based on the fact that Jesus came in the flesh and that the Holy Spirit will guide us.

Testing the Spirits through the Spiritual Gift of Discernment

The Holy Spirit has given certain believers in the church the gift of discernment to evaluate whether information that claims to be of God is satanic, human or divine. The word *discern* means to judge or evaluate. The central idea is to have the faculty for distinguishing between truth and error. This gift is particularly associated with prophecy and the ability to discern whether a prophecy is of God or a false prophet.

For example, Agnes was an active, radiant Christian, whose twenty-eight-year-old married son had a nervous breakdown. She decided to attend a healing meeting that was advertised in the newspaper. When the altar call was given she went forward to pray for her son. The faith healer asked why she had come forward. She explained her son's condition to him.

He said, "I have a prophecy from the Lord to give to you. Your son will be healed if you will believe."

She came home with enthusiasm. However, what she didn't realize was that the faith healer placed the whole responsibility of her son's healing upon her faith. After several weeks with her son's condition still remaining the same, Agnes' radiance disappeared and turned into depression. She stopped attending church.

One evening I went to visit her. She was in her chair, rocking back and forth and staring into space. She was in a catatonic state. Later she was admitted to a psychiatric ward of a state institution where she received shock therapy.

Our congregation prayed for Agnes. I made repeated visits to read Scripture and pray with her. At one point, the elders and I anointed her with oil and prayed for her. Eventually she recovered. Her son was also admitted to the institution and through prayer and biblical counseling, recovered, too.

I often wondered how many other lives were broken by this false prophet. Our verse tells us that "many false prophets have gone out into the world" (1 John 4:1). Scripture also says that their number will increase before the return of Christ (Matthew 24:3-5, 11). The spiritual gift of discernment is God's gift to the church to protect it from error and falsehood and the harm done by false prophets.

Boil in Oil

Emma was a woman I personally led to Christ along with her husband. Both became members of our church. About a year later, she became convinced that she was a prophetess. After counseling with Emma one day, I firmly believed she didn't have that gift.

She said, "The Lord told me that you wouldn't agree with me and not to believe you."

Later, Emma told some of our church people to be sure to attend prayer meeting on a designated date because the Lord had given her a message for our congregation. Emma told them that she had written the message on a piece of paper as the Lord spoke to her.

I heard of her plans to read the message. When Emma arrived I asked her to let me see it first. It was written in graphic language. The Lord would boil in oil the members of the congregation who didn't obey this message. I would not permit her to read the message because I believed it was a satanic attack against us.

Later, I phoned Pastor Paul Kenyon, who had the spiritual gift of discernment and was experienced with demonic activity. He consented to meet with the lady. The husband, however, wouldn't permit her to be tested by Kenyon. She, along with several other families, left the church. I continued to minister to the remaining families. Within a year our congregation tripled in size.

Discerning Demonic Traits in Emma

Emma's behavior and activities, when taken as a whole, demonstrated demonism.

1. *She was filled with pride.* Her attitude reflected pride and boldness through the entire experience. It was pride that led to the fall of Satan along with a host of angels.
2. *She had a problem with submission.* She refused the testing of spirits and spiritual help.
3. *She rejected the truth of God's Word.* She rejected biblical counseling and exchanged the truth of God for a lie.
4. *She wrote extra-biblical revelations.* Automatic writing of non-biblical truths was a dead giveaway of demonic intrusion.
5. *There was a lack of repentance and forgiveness.* Emma and her husband refused to repent and ask forgiveness. They never showed remorse, never wrote, then finally left the church.

Beware of False Doctrine

> The Spirit clearly says that in later times some will abandon the faith and follow deceiving spirits and things taught by demons. (1 Timothy 4:1)

Neil Anderson names groups and activities associated with false doctrines and demons along with a method of deliverance which has been successful.

Non-Christian Spiritual Experience Inventory

Circle any of the following activities in which you have been involved in any way.

Occult	Cult	Other Religions
Astral projection	Christian Science	Zen Buddhism
Ouija board	Unity	Hare Krishna
Table lifting	Scientology	Bahaism
Speaking in a trance	The Way International	Rosicrucianism
Automatic writing	Unification Church	Science of Mind
Visionary dreams	Church of the Living Word	Science of Creative Intelligence
Telepathy	Mormonism	Hinduism
Ghosts	Jehovah's Witnesses	Transcendental Meditation
Materialization	Children of God	Yoga
Clairvoyance	Swedenborgianism	Eckankar
Clairsentience	Unitarianism	Roy Masters
Fortune-telling	New Age	Silva Mind Control
Tarot cards	Other ________	Father Divine
Palm-reading		Theosophical Society
Astrology		Islam
Rod and pendulum (dowsing)		Black Muslim
Amateur hypnosis		Other ________ [2]
Healing magnetism		
Magic charming		
Mental suggestion		
Black & white magic		
Blood pacts		
Fetishism		
Incubi and succubi (sexual spirits)		

Taken from: *The Bondage Breaker* by Neil T. Anderson.

As you go through the list, pray in the following way:

Dear heavenly Father, I ask You to reveal to me all the occult practices, false religions and false teachers with which I have knowingly or unknowingly been involved.

Write down everything God brings to mind. After you are sure your list is complete, pray the following for each practice, religion and teacher:

Lord, I confess that I have participated in ______.
I ask Your forgiveness, and I renounce ________
as a counterfeit to true Christianity.

It is advisable to read Neil Anderson's book *The Bondage Breaker* to get acquainted with his methodology.

Trouble with Tongues

Becky was a member of a church I pastored. She wanted God's will for her life and became interested in the gifts of the Spirit. She looked at the list of the gifts in First Corinthians 12:28 and noted that they appeared to be listed by priority. "Apostleship" was first on the priority list and "gift of tongues" was last. At that point, her reasoning was as follows: "The gift of tongues is on the bottom of the list and therefore of least importance. I don't want the Lord to think that I'm proud, so I'm not going to ask for the best. I'll just humbly claim the least gift, the gift of tongues, as my spiritual gift." Becky claimed the gift and tried to speak in tongues, but nothing happened.

She prayed and tried again, to no avail. Trying to exercise faith, Becky said, "If I believe, then I shall receive the gift." She waited patiently, but after a few weeks nothing happened. Soon she lost the joy of the Lord.

What began as a serious attempt to find her spiritual gift eventually turned into a nightmare of depression. Becky's devotional and spiritual life slid rapidly into the pit of despair. After a few months she became suicidal. Satanic oppression was winning the battle over her spiritual well being.

Then Becky read the twelfth chapter of First Corinthians again. This time the eleventh verse shone as a bright beacon into her darkened and depressed mind. She read it again, particularly the phrase, "and he gives them to each one, *just as he determines*" (emphasis added). This key verse of Scripture put her back on spiritual track. She recognized it was His decision as the sovereign Lord to give gifts. She confessed her sin of playing God and dictating to Him what gift she chose. This powerful verse delivered her from her depression and suicidal tendencies. She regained the joy of the Lord. Later, she discovered her spiritual gift was the gift of serving.

Discerning and Dealing with False Tongues

While no one should deny the validity of the authentic gift of tongues, the inordinate pursuit of the tongues gift often opens the door for demons to enter people and hold them in bondage to falsehood and deception. This is a worldwide problem which confronts many believers who want to know how to test the manifestations to see whether or not they are of God.

A believer in England wrote the following paragraph in a letter mailed to me:

> I got to know about you through your book, *Find and Use Your Spiritual Gifts*. . . . I am writing to you because I need your help. . . . If a person is speaking in tongues and keeps on repeating the same phrase over and over, can I say that it is false? I was listening to a sister speaking in a tongue and these are the words that she kept on repeating, "he-ah, a-san-doh-lah." Please help me, Pastor Packo, because I believe that a lot of people are using false tongues.

I answered his letter and gave the following advice:

1. Pray and speak to your pastor or elder who may have the spiritual gift of discernment.
2. Tongues need to be interpreted. If not, they could be words of blasphemy or babble; or they could be vain repetition. What good is babbling? Read First Corinthians 14:28.
3. True tongues glorify Jesus and edify the church. The ministry of the Holy Spirit is to glorify Jesus. Read John 16:14.
4. When confronting the person, ask, "Has Jesus Christ come in the flesh?" Be careful not to say, "Do you believe in Jesus?" Jesus could refer to any person. You could receive a "yes" reply and be deceived.
5. Address the spirit with the following question: "Spirit, has Jesus Christ come in the flesh?" (Read First John 4:1-4). A false spirit will generally evade the question and try to sidestep the main issue. Be persistent. It may take time. If you receive a "no" answer, address the spirit in this fashion: "Spirit, in the name of Jesus Christ, the Son of God, I command you to flee!"

I concluded the letter encouraging him to share the advice with his pastor.

Here is an example of the power of positional thinking working together with the authority of the believer. It took place at a home Bible study that I attended. Halfway through the study one of the ladies interrupted Pastor Bussey and began to speak boldly and rapidly in a tongue. She swayed back and forth in a trancelike state.

Bussey asked for an interpretation. When none was given, he asked us to pray.

He then faced the lady and spoke to the spirit, saying, "Has Jesus Christ come in the flesh?"

After a brief hesitation the spirit said, "No."

Bussey then rebuked Satan and cast out the demon.

At once, the lady began to praise Jesus Christ and we all joined together in worship and praise. We sensed the awesome power of God behind the authority of the believer exercised over the demonic forces of the devil!

An outstanding example of a deliverance ministry to test the gift of speaking in tongues was exercised by the late Archie E. Ruark. According to the research of K. Neill Foster, Ruark was the first to apply the First John 4:1–4 passage to the testing of the gift of speaking in tongues. Ruark believed that tongues is one of the most frequent entry points for Satan in his attack upon Christians. After fifty-five years of ministry Ruark concluded that about ninety percent of all the tongues manifestations he had ever encountered had been false.[3]

A penetrating question is this: "If the modern-day tongues movement is genuine, why do the manifestations break down when Christian workers submit to the Ruark Procedure? Foster writes the following alarming words:

> Are millions and millions around the world being deceived by an alternate Jesus? Some in the tongues testing movement have been given to repeating details of the manifestations and multiplying the accounts of demons. . . . Building any kind of theology on utterances from the counter kingdom has to be the depth of foolishness. Though Origen was one of the first universalists, he had sense enough to say that we should never become "listeners to" or disciples of the demons.[4] *

Greater Is He That Is in You

Here is a verse of Scripture that provides great comfort and assurance to the child of God: "You, dear children, are from God and have overcome them, because the one who is in you is greater than the one who is in the world" (1 John 4:4). God the Holy Spirit, the Spirit of Truth, is with the true believer (John 15:26). He guides us into all truth that originates from the Word of God. To the nonbeliever, this is foolish because they are blinded by the world system that is under the domination of Satan and his demonic armies. These same evil forces are against us as Christians and are bent on our destruction. Satan wants us to go down in defeat, but our power is in Christ, for "greater is he that is in you, than he that is in the world" (1 John 4:4, KJV).

* (Check the endnotes and bibliography under "Elio Cuccaro" for the book title if you desire more information.)

SEVEN

Four Powerful Weapons to Defeat Destructive Thinking

Worship the LORD in the splendor of his holiness; tremble before him, all the earth. (Psalm 96:9)

True worship of God must be a constant and consistent attitude or state of mind within the believer. It will always be a sustained and blessed acknowledgment of love and adoration, subject in this life to degrees of perfection and intensity.[1]

—A.W. Tozer

Positional Thinker's Action #7

"I have taken the garment of praise, the shield of faith, the confident expectation of hope and the love of God to defeat destructive thoughts."

Praise, along with faith, hope and love are four powerful weapons to defeat destructive thinking. Praise needs to be that "consistent attitude and state of mind within the believer" to rise above tough circumstances. Chapters 7 and 8 present six warfare weapons to confront twenty-four damages that are listed in chapters ten through thirteen.

Weapon One: Praise Defeats Destructive Thinking

> Praise be to the God and Father of our Lord Jesus Christ, who has blessed us in the heavenly realms with every spiritual blessing in Christ. (Ephesians 1:3)

Neill Foster writes in his book *Warfare Weapons*, "Praise is really an assault weapon against Satan. If evil comes, praise the Lord: not for the evil, but as a declaration of war against it."[2] Foster then shares the following testimony and challenge.

> For instance, sometimes thoughts hit me which I recognize to be straight from the devil's pit. My reaction is "Praise the Lord!" But am I praising the Lord Jesus Christ for those horrid thoughts? Most assuredly not! With praise I go to war and the devil backs off. It is a great remedy. Try it.[3]

The Spiritual Benefits of Praise

There are three major spiritual benefits of praise which are available to all believers.

1. *Protection.* Praise directed to God pleases Him and protects us from our archenemy. God has ordained that everything we are and do should flow out of worship to Him as blessed by-products. The devil can't stand the believer who mirrors the glory of God with praise.
2. *Stimulation.* Praise transforms our personalities, which in turn builds our relationships, our service and our total lives as believers. In Warren Wiersbe's book *Real Worship*, he writes:

   > Worship means "a release of energy." It puts into life something which steps it up to a higher voltage. Through worship man comes to God at first, and has an immediate experience with God and goes forth transformed and stimulated to new levels of endeavor.[4]

   Thus, it is evident that worship defeats destructive thinking by releasing a "high voltage" energy which transforms and stimulates us to greater ventures of faith.
3. *Transformation.* Praise also helps to transform us into Christlikeness.

   > And we, who with unveiled faces all reflect the Lord's glory, are being transformed into his likeness with ever-increasing glory, which comes from the Lord, who is the Spirit. (2 Corinthians 3:18)

When Moses came down from Mount Sinai his face was like a mirror, reflecting the glory of God. Moses placed a veil over his face so the people wouldn't see the glory fade away. We, however, instead of veiling our faces, want the world to see what the grace of God can do through us. The more we declare God's glory through praise, the more we will reflect and mirror Jesus.

Weapon Two: Faith Defeats Destructive Thinking

> In addition to all this, take up the shield of faith, with which you can extinguish all the flaming arrows of the evil one. (Ephesians 6:16)

Faith in the power of God will defeat any destructive thought resulting in victory. Ephesians 6:16 is introduced to demonstrate the flexibility of faith against the flaming arrows of the evil one. Both the Old and New Testaments show the shield of faith as God's protection for the believer. The shield is referred to in the first war recorded in the Bible after Abram defeated the four kings and rescued his nephew Lot. The Lord spoke to Abram in a vision: "Do not be afraid, Abram. I am your shield, your very great reward" (Genesis 15:1). What an amazing revelation! Believers from the very beginning have been instructed not to fear the enemy, for God is our shield.

Paul commands the Christian, "take up the shield of faith" (Ephesians 6:16). When we pick up the shield and use it we have God's protection. Without it, we are defenseless against the fiery arrows of destructive thoughts and temptations that Satan hurls our way. Faith is appropriating Christ for every battle. It is our shield that deflects Satan's arrows. His fiery darts generally rain upon the believer. We commonly express it with either "when it rains it pours" or "troubles come in bushel baskets."

Faith is vital for there are many things we cannot do without it:

1. Be saved (John 3:36);
2. Have peace with God (Romans 5:1);
3. Please God (Hebrews 11:6);
4. Pray effectively (James 1:6);
5. Have joy (1 Peter 1:5-6); or
6. Live victoriously (1 John 5:14).

Furthermore, the Bible stresses that we are to live by the faith of the Son of God (Galatians 2:20) and warns us that "everything that does not come from faith is sin" (Romans 14:23). Let us not be kept off guard. Victory doesn't come by having our minds preoccupied with the enemy, seeing him under every bush. Rather, "[l]et us fix our eyes on Jesus, the author and perfecter of our faith" (Hebrews 12:2). This arouses enthusiasm and energy in the fight. "[I]n all these things we are more than conquerors through him who loved us" (Romans 8:37).

Weapon Three: Hope Defeats Destructive Thinking

> And now these three remain: faith, hope and love. But the greatest of these is love. (1 Corinthians 13:13)

Hope ranks second only to love in the above verse. Love is the greatest, for it will continue in eternity. Faith and hope will end when we see Christ, for they will finally be realized. But for now, hope is a necessary spiritual weapon to smash the old sinful nature's addiction for hopelessness. People in this state do not expect a favorable outcome. They are so despondent that they don't feel like receiving any help toward recovery.

When a Christian begins to feel hopelessness, this distress must be replaced by enthusiastic hope. Hope, as used in the Bible, always denotes a confident expectation; it never carries the idea of uncertainty as it does in our English language (as when we say cautiously, "I hope so").

The positional thinker reckons the old sinful nature to be dead with its hopeless position. The gospel presents to us a double hope: 1) our future hope when Christ and the resurrection of the body will deliver our bodies from pain and tears. At that time we will receive our final spiritual, physical, psychological and social perfection. But there is hope for an abundant life right now; and 2) our present hope in Christ brings to us, in the times of stress, an abundant life of peace, comfort, joy and assurance. All of us need to be reminded of our hope in the gospel.

Perhaps an example would help clarify the situation. A man has just been diagnosed with diabetes. The physician tells him, "You have to take insulin by injection three times a day for the rest of your life." At this point, an emotional response of hopelessness can be experienced by the diabetic. This can increase if the person continues to have fatigue, blurred vision, constant thirst, muscle weakness, tingling and numbness in hands and feet.[5] Remember that hope produces endurance under trial. If the prognosis of your illness or accident may be life-threatening, take your weapon of hope and use it to encourage you. "For everything that was written in the past was written to teach us, so that through endurance and the encouragement of the Scriptures we might have hope" (Romans 15:4).

Weapon Four: God's Love Defeats Destructive Thinking

When a patient is diagnosed with a life-threatening disease, the psychological reaction hits the panic button which immediately questions God's love. "How can You love me when You have allowed me to contract this disease?" Our love for God cools down. Love is replaced by a host of fears such as the fear of the future and fear of death. We know from the Bible that these fears are not from God but are used by Satan to damage our love relationship with God. "For God has not given us a spirit of fear, but of power and of love and of a sound mind" (2 Timothy 1:7, NKJV).

The New Testament uses two words to describe love: 1) *Philia*—a loving behavior which builds a relationship within or outside the context of the family, and 2) *Agape*—the love of God. Agape love is a sacrificial love that is part of God's essential nature. The greatest example of God's love occurred when He sacrificed Himself on the cross to release those who believe from the bondage of sin and Satan. Sacrificial love is a badge of discipleship. True disciples of Christ are to love one another (John 13:34-35). If we love one another we will give rather than try to see what we can get. The proof of love is obedience. Jesus said, "If anyone loves Me, he will keep My word" (14:23, NKJV). Love is also the fruit of the Holy Spirit (Galatians 5:22). When a person is born again, the Holy Spirit comes to indwell and reaches out to love others.

We can overcome Satan, for "the one who is in you is greater than the one who is in the world" (1 John 4:4). The person who is spiritual is the Spirit-filled person. K. Neill Foster writes of thirteen weapons to use in spiritual warfare. The one weapon that rises above all others is love. He calls love "the super weapon."

> Love is the super weapon of the Christian, the weapon among all others in the Christian's arsenal which dwarfs all its competitors. . . . When a person is converted, or born again by the Spirit of God, the Holy Spirit becomes one with the human spirit. So every Christian has a love bomb within him! It is ready to explode, and given the proper circumstances it will. . . . There is no situation, no problem, no difficulty which cannot be conquered by love.[6]

Pray the following prayer if your love for Christ has cooled down due to your illness.

> Dear Heavenly Father,
>
> I worship and praise You for Your sacrificial love that sent Jesus to die in my place on the cross. Please forgive me for questioning Your love for me when I contracted my illness. I take up Your shield of faith to protect me. I count my sinful nature to be dead to sin but alive to God in Christ. I rejoice in the hope of the glory of God and I rest on the victory You won on the cross to defeat any attacks from the devil. I claim Your super weapon of love. I believe there is no situation, no problem, no difficulty that cannot be conquered by love.
>
> In Jesus' name, Amen.

EIGHT

Two Offensive Weapons to Defeat Destructive Thinking

. . . take the sword of the Spirit, which is the word of God. Pray at all times and on every occasion in the power of the Holy Spirit. Stay alert and be persistent in your prayers for all Christians everywhere. (Ephesians 6:17-18, NLT)

I believe many who bring the Word of God against seemingly impossible objects do not realize just how powerful God's Word is. Too many times they stop hammering just when the rock of circumstances is about to crumble before them. . . . Healing will not take place if we are equivocating. If we always preface our prayers with, "If it be Thy will . . . ," nothing will happen.[1]

—K. Neill Foster

Positional Thinker's Action #8

"I wield the Word as a sword that penetrates the heart, pray the Bible and pray in the Spirit to replace destructive thoughts with the positive thoughts of God's powerful Word."

Weapon Five: God's Positive Word Defeats Destructive Thinking

You may ask, "What is more important, prayer or the Word? I say to you, "What is more important, the left wing or the right wing of a fighter plane?" Both are necessary in battling the enemy. It is through the Word of God and prayer that the Holy Spirit empowers us to withstand any hurt or damage that Satan may hurl our way.

The Ephesian letter has transported us into the heavenly realm of positional thinking. After presenting this teaching, Paul makes one last plea: "Finally, be strong in the Lord and in his mighty power" (6:10). This is a call for military action against the devil's schemes. As he attempts to open the floodgates of physical, mental, social and psychological hurts, it is a challenge to put on God's full armor and take a stand against him. Our battle is against the spiritual forces of the dark world unleashed against us. The powerful sword of the Spirit, the Word of God, is our weapon: "For the word of God is living and active. Sharper than any double-edged sword, it penetrates even to dividing soul and spirit, joints and marrow; it judges the thoughts and attitudes of the heart" (Hebrews 4:12).

The Word of God is not a formal, dead, inactive book; it has a living energy that penetrates the heart. And when it does, it brings to light the real thoughts, feelings and motives of our souls. It awakens, converts and sanctifies us. As a surgeon's knife is used for the healing of the body, the truth of the Word heals the soul. It always produces just effects. I have experienced the healing Word of God in my own life and ministry and have seen its penetrating effects in the lives of thousands of people. Let me share a few.

Healing through the Powerful Word of God

I received a phone call from Bud, who lives in Vermont. He had contracted cancer over a year and a half ago and was in a state of remission. He attended self-help meetings in a congregational church. They had a small library of recommended reading. One was my *Coping with Cancer* book. After reading the evangelistic chapter, the sword of the Word awakened his soul and Bud was converted. He was elated. "The book is not only helping me cope with cancer," he said, "but also is helping me cope with my alcoholism. If I had received the Lord in the first place, I wouldn't be an alcoholic." The positive Word had changed his negative life.

Elaine attended our support group. She had an incurable blood disease. She was scheduled for dialysis. That Sunday she attended her church. The pastor concluded his message, saying, "If anyone is sick and desires to be anointed with oil and prayed for, please come forward."

Elaine's first reaction was reluctance. *I don't want to go forward in front of all of these people*, she said to herself. But before she knew it, she found herself moving. "I felt my body taking me forward," she said. She testified of the wonderful spiritual experience of being instructed in the Word, and being anointed and prayed for according to the instructions given in the book of James.

> Is any one of you sick? He should call the elders of the church to pray over him and anoint him with oil

> in the name of the Lord. And the prayer offered in faith will make the sick person well; the Lord will raise him up. If he has sinned, he will be forgiven. Therefore confess your sins to each other and pray for each other so that you may be healed. (5:14-16)

Later she was examined by her physician who announced, "You don't need dialysis anymore. Your whole blood chemistry has changed since your last test."

Life Spared through the Word of God

Mrs. Jean Lewis, who attended one of our support groups in Dayton, Ohio, told the following story of the Japanese attack on Pearl Harbor. Her husband Ethan was returning from maneuvers on the *USS Medusa*, a repair ship. It was due to berth alongside the *USS Arizona*. However, another ship, the *USS Utah*, had taken that spot. The *Medusa's* captain signaled the captain of the *Utah* that they had taken the *Medusa's* berth. Their captain signaled back asking permission to remain there over the weekend since they were to leave Pearl Harbor to return to the states on the morning of December 8. With ships that size, it was too difficult to maneuver around in the harbor. The *Medusa* took the assigned berth of the *Utah* and that is where it was at the time of the Pearl Harbor attack.

Early in the morning two days later Ethan Lewis was reading a newspaper. He heard explosions and remarked, "They don't practice on Sunday morning!" One of the sailors looked out the window and exclaimed, "Those planes have red balls on them!" It was the insignia of the Japanese so they knew they were under attack. He said if he put his arm out the window he could have touched those planes, they were so close.

Before their eyes, they saw ships all around them on fire and men swimming from one ship to another trying to escape. Ethan threw down the newspaper and grabbed his Bible and began reading and praying. So did the other men. They thought, *This is the end.*

Later, notebooks left by the Japanese recorded that they had wanted to bomb the big repair ship, the *USS Medusa*, which was always berthed alongside the *Arizona*. If the *Medusa* had been where it was supposed to be, it would have been hit and sunk. History books report that a mist was over the *Medusa* that morning. Six bombs were aimed at it, but not one hit. Ethan said, "Six bombs barely missed my ship at Pearl Harbor. Would one of the bombs have hit us if we had not been reading our Testaments and praying? It might have. I promised Jesus to follow Him."

Price was a middle-aged man who had came forward to be anointed with oil and prayed for. When I asked him what his problem was, he said, "I confess that I am a glutton." He also mentioned failing eyesight and a bad knee that gave him a sharp pain with every step he took, and made a clicking noise. The elders and I prayed for Price and anointed him with oil.

When we finished with anointing and praying for all the people at the altar, I went to the book table to join Elaine. Price came over and shared with me that he felt a warmth go down through his body when we prayed for him. He recognized immediately that the pain with the click completely left his leg as he walked to the table. Later he phoned the pastor and said that he had lost his appetite and only ate one-third of the amount of food he ordinarily ate. He said, "My eye problem is clearing up. I can read the newspaper and also can read signs at a distance for the first time in a long time." The pastor said that Price praised the Lord for the healing that was taking place in his body.

Weapon Six: Praying the Bible Defeats Destructive Thinking

We are instructed in Ephesians 6:18 to "[p]ray at all times and on every occasion in the power of the Holy Spirit" (NLT). I want us to concentrate on one kind of praying called praying the Bible. Praying the Bible is praying to God the promises He has given us for living a positive spiritual life. Praying the Bible is a powerful method of replacing our negative thoughts with the positive thoughts of the Word of God. When you are praying verses you are praying them into a pattern of thinking that reflects the positive. We are saying back to God what God says to us. We are personalizing the Word of God in our hearts. And because it is God's Word, we can pray it with authority.

In one of my healing meetings, a lady came forward to be anointed and prayed for. She was clutching her baby with fear in her eyes. She said that her mother had died of breast cancer and that her first daughter had also died. She was fearful that both she and her baby daughter would also soon die. I quoted this powerful verse to her: "For God has not given us a spirit of fear, but of power and of love and of a sound mind" (2 Timothy 1:7, NKJV).

"If the Lord didn't give you the spirit of fear, where did it come from?" I asked. "Did it come from God?"

"No," she answered.

Then I explained to her what was happening. "Satan, through your old sinful nature, is attacking your mind. God gives you power; He gives you love and He gives you a sound mind. Why don't you pray and claim this verse? Ask God's forgiveness and thank Him for His power, His love and for a sound mind. Replace the destructive fear with the positive Word of God."

She prayed the words of Scripture earnestly and with authority.

Then I anointed her with oil and prayed, "Satan, we take authority over you, and I command you in Jesus' name to stop attacking our sister's mind with fearful thoughts of death!"

Her fear disappeared and was replaced with the peace of God.

Praying the Scriptures with authority sets people free to experience the healing Word of God.

Four Things You Can Learn from Praying the Bible

1. If you cannot pray because you are trapped by destructive emotions such as fear, discouragement and doubt, praying the Scriptures will release in your heart positive faith to pray. "Faith comes by hearing, and hearing by the word of God" (Romans 10:17, NKJV).
2. If you read a promise, such as Second Timothy 1:7, meditate on it and pray the promise, you will be praying the will of God and replacing destructive thoughts with God's positive Word. Remember to rest in the victory you already have in Christ.
3. When you say back to God what God has said to you, you are already in communication with God. From

this point move into conversation with God about what is on your heart.
4. Remember point three, for Satan probably will return again with the same attack. After you bind him the thoughts will cease. Matthew 18:18 states: "I tell you the truth, whatever you bind on earth will be bound in heaven, and whatever you loose on earth will be loosed in heaven."

If you are interested in more information on binding, look in the bibliography for an excellent book by K. Neill Foster titled *Binding and Loosing*.

Example of Praying the Bible

The Psalms express every emotion. Read Psalm 103:1-5 and then pray it. It will break the inertia and create within you powerful thoughts of praise. Personalize the passage for ownership. In the example below, the added personalized words are italicized.

> Praise the LORD, O my soul;
> all my inmost being, *I* praise *Your* holy name.
> Praise the LORD, O my soul,
> and *I will* not forget all *Your* benefits—
> *You* forgive all *my* sins
> and heal all *my* diseases.
> *You who* redeems *my* life from the pit
> and crowns *me* with love and compassion,
> *You Lord* who satisfies *my* desires with good things
> so that *my* youth is renewed like the eagle's.
> [*I praise you.*] (103:1-5, author's paraphrase)

Then petition the Lord for your specific needs and pray as He directs you. Praying the Bible defeats negative thinking in a powerful way. It blasts away negative, destructive thoughts that Satan tries to implant in our minds. When the Word of God fills our minds, there is no room for devilish thoughts.

NINE

Practicing Positional Thinking in Tough Circumstances

Since, then, you have been raised with Christ, set your hearts on things above, where Christ is seated at the right hand of God. Set your minds on things above, not on earthly things. For you died, and your life is now hidden with Christ in God. (Colossians 3:1-3)

In contrast to the popular exhortation to "keep looking up" (from ourselves to Christ), we are to "keep looking down (from our position in Him) upon our circumstances on earth."[1]

—Miles J. Stanford

Positional Thinker's Action #9

"I am practicing positional thinking to prevent getting crushed under tough circumstances which results in a greater potential for physical, social, spiritual and psychological damage."

In the next four chapters, we will deal with the physical, spiritual, psychological and social reactions of persons who are going through tough circumstances. These may include life-threatening diseases such as cancer or heart disease, or a damaged or twisted body from an auto accident. These afflictions require immediate medical attention. The physical pain often triggers psychological, spiritual and social damage to the whole person. While the treatment is taking place the power of positional thinking sets our minds above where our life is hidden with Christ in God.

Getting Crushed under Your Tough Circumstance?

A pastor, visiting one of his members in the hospital, asked, "How are you doing?"

"Not very well, under these circumstances," replied the patient.

"That is your main problem," the pastor quickly answered. "As a Christian, you should be living *above* your circumstances, not *under* them."

To reduce damage to our total being when we are faced with tough circumstances, we need to practice positional thinking. In this way, we by faith take our seat in the heavenly realms *above* those things that would crush us.

I thank the Lord for this "positional" truth that strengthened me in coping with the physical, spiritual, psychological and social damages of cancer. I also thank Him for His daily healing touches to my body.

How did I practice the power of positional thinking? By beginning the morning with prayer. Part of that prayer was this: "Lord Jesus, thank You for Your death and resurrection for me. I count my old self to be dead with Your death and my new self to be alive through Your resurrection. As I take my seat with You in the heavenlies, I claim Your resurrection power for this day."

Whenever I experienced an unusual amount of physical pain, such as the "night sweats" or the bouts of violent nausea, my prayer would be, "Lord Jesus, I take Your resurrection life for my body. May Your life flow through this body of mine for a special quickening touch."

On many such occasions, my wife, Elaine would be there to agree together with me in believing prayer for healing.

Disease Can Be Inflicted by the Devil

In some instances of diseases mentioned in the Bible neither God nor Satan are mentioned. Note the Shunammite couple's son (2 Kings 4:18-21) and Naaman's leprosy (5:1). In the case of the man blind from birth (John 9:1), disease was inflicted to bring glory to God. Though the disciples blamed his blindness on sin, Jesus said, "Neither this man nor his parents sinned, . . . but this happened so that the work of God might be displayed in his life" (9:3).

However, we know that disease can be inflicted by Satan, as seen in the familiar story of Job, alluded to in chapter 4. The New Testament gives two examples of Satan afflicting persons. Luke describes Jesus healing a woman severely "bent over" and unable to stand erect, "whom Satan [had] kept bound for eighteen long years" (Luke

13:16). The apostle Paul had "a thorn in [his] flesh, a messenger of Satan, to torment [him]" (2 Corinthians 12:7).

God in His divine plan sent Jesus to this sin-cursed earth "to destroy the devil's work" (1 John 3:8). For that reason Jesus died. For that reason He rose from the dead. For that reason He will return to complete His work in us, giving us glorified spirits, souls and bodies.

Satan Uses Sickness to Bring Spiritual Defeat

Satan can use illnesses to bring spiritual defeat even when he did not inflict them in the first place. He uses these discomforting ills to discourage us. In this way, he wages spiritual warfare against sick believers. His avenue of attack is through our sinful natures passed down to us from Adam and Eve in the Garden of Eden. These natures are a reflection of Satan's own evil nature.

Even though believers have a new nature, it is still possible to let the thinking of our old sinful natures gain control of our minds. This is evident when we allow a flood of destructive emotions such as fear of the future, poor self worth, depression and bitterness to gain control. We who have experienced a serious disease such as cancer can understand the battle between our two inner natures that can bring out the worst in us. Our thoughts are a reflection of either our old nature or our new nature.

How do we cope with this spiritual warfare within us? As we mentioned in chapter 2, God wants us to rest in the victory already won by His Son. When Satan attacks our rest through a tough circumstance, we should pray,

"Lord, I'm facing a difficult situation. The devil is trying to defeat me. I praise You that I already have the victory."

Our Threefold Positional Thinking

When grappling with the two inner natures, practice threefold positional thinking:

1. Think co-crucifixion. Think "death position" to the old sinful nature. Count your old sinful nature dead with Christ's death.
2. Think co-resurrection. Think "risen life position" of the new nature. Count your new nature alive with Christ's resurrection.
3. Think co-seated. Think of sitting together with Christ in heaven. From this position Jesus has delegated to us the authority of the believer. This position assures us of victory over our sinful nature, the world and the devil.

Positional thinkers trust in the supernatural healing power of God to supplement their doctor's treatments. They trust God to lead them to the best, most reliable treatments, knowing that God in His sovereignty uses doctors as instruments of healing. In the final analysis, though, it is the Lord God who heals. Doctors can prescribe medication or perform surgery, and psychologists can give counsel in dealing with the emotions, but the Lord heals.

In the next four chapters I make use of medical and psychological advice that is brief, but helpful. You may ask the question, "What has this to do with spiritual warfare?" Satan is gleeful when we deny such advice, for he is bent on our spiritual, physical and psychological destruction.

Our threefold positional thinking, based on our victory in Christ, comes to our rescue when we appropriate it by counting the victory of Christ as complete.

Six Powerful Weapons to Defeat Destructive Thinking

This acrostic, W-E-A-P-O-N, will help you remember the six powerful weapons of warfare needed to defeat destructive thinking as discussed in chapters 7 and 8. As you apply these weapons and become a positional thinker, you will rejoice greatly in the Lord during your tough circumstance rather than have a pity party. With these six powerful weapons in deployment, your destructive thoughts will flee and be replaced by those that are positive and biblical.

A Review of the Six Weapons to Defeat Destructive Thinking

W - Word of God	The Word of God is called the sword of the Spirit. It penetrates the heart, brings to light and judges the thoughts and attitudes of the heart.
E - Exercise Faith	Faith in the victory we already have in Christ will defeat destructive thoughts resulting in renewed vigor.
A - A Life of Praise	Praise and worship of God satisfies our spirit, reflects His glory to those around us and routs the archenemy of our souls.

P - Praying the Bible	Praying the Bible is praying to God His Word which strengthens, matures and keeps us on the offensive in spiritual warfare.
O - Ongoing Hope	Hope produces endurance under trials. It is a confident expectation in Christ who gives abundant life now, and a future life in heaven that has no pain.
N - Need God's Love	God's love is the Christian's superweapon. There is no problem or difficulty which cannot be conquered by love.[2]

TEN

How Positional Thinkers Deal with Physical Damage

He himself bore our sins in his body on the tree, so that we might die to sins and live for righteousness; by his wounds you have been healed. (1 Peter 2:24)

Think of the multiple benefits. The Christian has received God-given physical and spiritual procedures for healthy living. The Christian experiences the inward assistance of the Holy Spirit. God's indwelling presence enables him to obey God's health-giving, spirit-maturing teachings. God's indwelling presence also sustains him in sickness. The unsaved have only human and material help. The Christian has all of the earthly helps, but over and beyond all these, the believer has the presence, the promises and the provisions of His Heavenly Father.[1]

—Robert G. Witty

Positional Thinker's Action #10

"To overcome the potential for greater physical damage, I trust in the supernatural healing power of God to supplement my doctor's treatments and will use the six warfare weapons to rout destructive thinking."

In this chapter, we will discuss six of the numerous physical damages that may occur from serious illness. With each one will be brief but helpful advice, along with positive Bible verses for us to pray. While this information is helpful for both believer and nonbeliever, remember that the born-again Christian has the added advantage of a loving heavenly Father who has given us His presence, promises and provisions. The believer also has the position of authority that gives him positive assurance as he copes with physical damage.

However, despite God's provision for those who are ill, we must still face the onslaught of Satan. The devil will use the arrows of physical pain, an unhealthy immune system, mouth and throat problems, a decreased blood count, high blood pressure and loss of energy that comes from our illnesses to wear us down. Slyly he worms his way through our illnesses to deceive us. He also tries to stir up our old sinful nature to think destructive thoughts of doubt, disbelief and denial that will hinder any kind of healing.

How do you as a positional thinker handle this "old sinful nature" kind of thinking? By practicing positional thinking from your seat of authority in the heavenly realms. Think of the devil's defeat through Christ's death, resurrection and ascension. Think co-crucifixion, co-resurrection and co-seated with Christ. Practice sanctification. Take your weapons of praise, faith, hope, love, God's Word and prayer to dispel the destructive thoughts that loom up from your old sinful nature. This will clear the way for the manner in which God will heal you.

Arrow Number One: Physical Pain

When pain occurs, it is almost always manageable. You need to describe the pain to your doctor accurately in order to manage it effectively. Your doctor doesn't know how severe the pain is until he is told. With this in mind, keep a notepad on hand to jot down thoughts and feelings so you will have accurate information next time you visit his office.

There are three important points about medication and pain control presented in the book *I Can Cope*:

1. The medication must be equal to the pain. There are three types of pain: mild, moderate, and severe pain. And there are three classifications of drugs for mild, moderate, and severe pain. Taking a drug designed for mild pain when you are experiencing severe pain is like using a squirt gun on a house fire. No amount of the medication will be able to touch the pain. Be honest and specific about the degree of pain you experience. Otherwise, the prescribed drug may be inappropriate.
2. Medication must be taken before the pain becomes intense. Many people tend to "tough it out" and wait until the pain gets really bad before taking the medication. Once the pain has traveled from the original site through all the nerve receptors in the body and into the brain, it takes a long time for medication to reverse that cycle. For most people, it is best to take medication on a regular schedule, around the clock to prevent the pain cycle from starting.

3. Morphine is no longer considered a "last effort" drug; it is the drug of choice for chronic, severe pain. It is a myth that morphine use always leads to addiction. . . . [T]he chemical make-up of oral morphine closely resembles the body's own pain killing endorphins. When pain becomes less severe, the person's need for the drug automatically decreases. This is true in normal nonaddictive personalities.[2]

The right drug in the right dose given at the right time relieves eighty-five to ninety percent of pain. People who are knowledgeable about their pain and assertive enough to ask for what they need can achieve an acceptable level of pain control over long periods of time.

◆ PRAY THE FOLLOWING SCRIPTURE:

> To keep me from becoming conceited because of these surpassingly great revelations, there was given me a thorn in my flesh, a messenger of Satan, to torment me. Three times I pleaded with the Lord to take it away from me. But he said to me, "My grace is sufficient for you, for my power is made perfect in weakness." Therefore I will boast all the more gladly about my weaknesses, so that Christ's power may rest on me. That is why, for Christ's sake, I delight in weaknesses, in insults, in hardships, in persecutions, in difficulties. For when I am weak, then I am strong. (2 Corinthians 12:7-10) ◆

Arrow Number Two: The Depressed Immune System

If 100 people were suddenly exposed to some virus, many would become ill, while others would not. The difference hinges on the immune system. The immune systems of the ones who became ill would be unhealthy, while those of the others would be healthy and more active. We say they have better resistance. Every disease, whether a cold or cancer, is resisted by the immune system. It brings together the body's total response to illness.

How do you build a stronger immune system? There are four ingredients.

1. Exercise is needed for building a good immune system. The average American does not exercise consistently.
2. Rest and relaxation are essential. We are a stressed-out society. When we do take a vacation and later return home, we are more tired than before we left.
3. A positive mental attitude that is cheerful and optimistic about life is important.
4. Nutrition is vital. Many processed foods are aimed at our fast-paced lifestyle. Nutrients, which are needed by our immune system, are removed or destroyed for the sake of convenience and ease of preparation. It is recommended to take a one-a-day multiple vitamin and eat healthy, fresh foods.

Dr. B.B. Miller writes,

> A survey of American eating habits shows the inadequacy of our food choices. The number one source of calories is white bread and crackers; number two is doughnuts and cookies; number three is alcohol. The number one and two meat sources are hot dogs and luncheon meats. Soft drinks supply one half of our carbohydrates.[3]

Do you realize that more than 30 million new white blood cells and over 3 million antibody molecules are produced in your body in a ten-minute period? This is not the kind of system to try to run on doughnuts, cola and cookies.

Another way to build our immune system is by filling our minds with biblical thoughts. For years medical and psychological researchers largely ignored the impact of faith and spiritual well-being on physical health. Today's thinking in this area is revolutionary, because doctors have discovered that spiritual life does have a powerful influence on health and healing. Sugar and pills simply are not enough.

A study of 1,718 older adults in North Carolina found that blood levels of the undesirable immune system protein interleukin-6 (IL-6) were lower in people over age sixty-five who attended church services at least once a week. Dr. Marcia Ory, chief of social science research on aging at the National Institute on Aging, said, "It's incredibly significant, because it's one of the very first studies that tries to look at the biological linkages." Dr. Harold Loenig, a Duke psychiatrist and lead author of the study said, "Those who go to church or synagogue regularly are physically healthier, mentally healthier and they have healthier immune systems."[4] Thus, to boost your immune system, we need to reactivate our spiritual lives and increase our meditation on Scripture. By filling our thoughts with prayer and Scripture, we can battle chronic illness and life-threatening disease.

PRAY THE FOLLOWING SCRIPTURE:

My son, pay attention to what I say;
listen closely to my words.
Do not let them out of your sight,
keep them within your heart;

for they are life to those who find them
and health to a man's whole body.
(Proverbs 4:20-22)

Arrow Number Three: Mouth and Throat

Treatments such as chemotherapy cause mouth and throat problems, which I discovered firsthand. Following chemotherapy I developed several canker sores in the top of my throat that were so painful I couldn't even talk. It was impossible to eat without severe pain. This lasted for a period of one week; then would disappear until my next treatment. The oncologist prescribed a medication to relieve the pain temporarily when I ate. Ice cream, popsicles and milk shakes became favorites during those temporary periods of painful canker sores.

Here are some simple ways to deal with mouth and throat problems:

- Avoid highly acidic foods, such as oranges and pizza.
- Don't drink grapefruit, pineapple and orange juice.
- Use a straw to make drinking easier.
- Soak foods in your beverage before eating.
- Suck on sugarless candy or ice chips.

How do you relieve a bitter or metallic taste in your mouth? I had a metallic taste for over six months during the whole period of treatments. Chaplain Weimer, when he was chaplain of the Franciscan Medical Center in Dayton, Ohio, told our support group meeting how his wife, Sharon, had experienced the metallic taste after her radiation treatments. They experimented with different foods. Hot, spicy foods were out. Cool foods became more palatable. If you are having this difficulty, eat foods cold or at room temperature. They'll taste better. If red meat doesn't taste right, substitute chicken, turkey, eggs or dairy products. Drink more liquids. Be creative.

PRAY THE FOLLOWING SCRIPTURE:

Then they cried to the LORD in their trouble,
and he saved them from their distress.
He sent forth his word and healed them;
he rescued them from the grave.
Let them give thanks to the LORD for his unfailing love
and his wonderful deeds for men.
(Psalm 107:19-21)

Arrow Number Four: Blood Count Decrease

Radiation can be hard on bone marrow and blood counts. In most cases, these side effects will be temporary, but very high dosages of radiation may result in permanent tissue damage. In the vast majority of cases, the benefits of radiotherapy far outweigh the disadvantages, and recent developments have eliminated many former problems. Today's radiation therapists can deliver treatment with greater accuracy and fewer side effects than ever before. In fact, radiation therapy can be so effective that it is sometimes called "surgery without a knife."

Both surgery and radiation, however, have their limitations. Chemotherapy is one of those methods used to treat cancers that have spread to more than one place in the body. The word is a shortened form of "chemical therapy." "Chemo" is an even shorter term.

Chemo attacks not only the cancer cells, but also the red bone marrow where blood cells are made. This is why doctors closely monitor the amounts of both white and red blood cells, as well as platelets. Decreased numbers of any type of blood cell (low blood counts) can lead to such difficulties as infection, weakness, abnormal bleeding tendencies and shortness of breath. The good news is that blood counts return to near normal in most cases.

Blood cells and platelets play an important role in our bodies in protecting us from infection. The white blood cells fight infectious bacteria. A decrease in white blood cell counts makes people more susceptible. During times when the blood count is low, we need to wash our hands often, avoid crowds and keep away from people with colds and coughs. If you cut or scrape your skin, wash it immediately. If you like to garden, wear gloves, as there are many organisms living in the soil.

Red blood cells carry oxygen to all parts of the body. A decrease in the red blood cell count can result in anemia. If the count gets too low, the doctor may advise having a blood transfusion. You may need to rest more and to move more slowly to adapt to the decrease of oxygen in your blood.

Platelets help the blood to clot. If the count is low a person may bleed or bruise more easily. Use cotton swabs to clean your teeth instead of a toothbrush. Avoid contact sports. Report any unusual bruising or bleeding to your doctor. A transfusion of platelets may be necessary if the count gets too low.

PRAY THE FOLLOWING SCRIPTURE:

And a woman was there who had been subject to bleeding for twelve years. She had suffered a great deal under the care of many doctors and had spent all she had, yet instead of getting better she grew worse. When she heard about Jesus, she came up behind him in the crowd and touched his cloak, because she thought, "If I just touch his clothes, I will be healed." Immediately her bleeding stopped and she felt in her body that she was freed from her suffering. . . .

He said to her, "Daughter, your faith has healed you. Go in peace and be freed from your suffering." (Mark 5:25-29, 34)

Arrow Number Five: High Blood Pressure

Studies show that those who experience chronic stress on the job are three times as likely to develop high blood pressure.

Evidence is mounting that the reduction of sodium intake can have a significant effect on blood pressure. Several studies have also shown that you can lower your blood pressure by taking extra calcium. In one study, more than half of the women and a third of the men shaved more than ten points off their systolic blood pressure by taking extra calcium.[5]

Researchers, using high-tech monitors, have discovered that happiness caused systolic blood pressure to drop, while anxiety caused diastolic pressure to rise.

PRAY THE FOLLOWING SCRIPTURE:

Rejoice in the Lord always. I will say it again: Rejoice! Let your gentleness be evident to all. The

> Lord is near. Do not be anxious about anything, but in everything, by prayer and petition, with thanksgiving, present your requests to God. And the peace of God, which transcends all understanding, will guard your hearts and your minds in Christ Jesus. (Philippians 4:4-7) ◆

Arrow Number Six: Loss of Energy

Life with any kind of serious illness can be exhausting. A person's energy level varies from day to day and week to week. The key is to work smarter, not harder.

How do you conserve personal energy?

1. Lower your expectations. Don't try to keep up at your old pace. It can only lead to frustration. If you are accustomed to keeping a spotless house, lower your expectations to simply having an uncluttered house. If you mowed the lawn once a week, settle on twice a month.
2. Make a "To Do List" each day. Prioritize the list. Start with things that *must* be done. Finish your list with things that are pleasant to do. By starting a list, you can avoid wasting time on unimportant activities at the expense of those that *are* important. Among the "musts" is at least one activity that is purely for your pleasure such as a trip to the library, lunch with a friend or watching your favorite television program.
3. Balance work with rest. Knowing when to stop can mean the difference between a good day and a tiring day. Analyze your day and pace yourself so the work is equal to your energy level. Do heavier tasks, like house cleaning, when energy is high, and save lighter tasks like letter writing for rest time.

4. Strive to simplify. The less you have to contend with, the more you can get done. Learn to say "no" to time-wasting, nonproductive activities. It is important to put all your energy into getting well.
5. Don't be afraid to ask for help. If you don't have the energy to do a particular project, feel free to ask family and friends to help. Take a big step and ask someone to scrub your floors, mow your lawn or clean your refrigerator. By learning to ask others for help, you are able to save a tremendous amount of energy.

PRAY THE FOLLOWING SCRIPTURE:

Is any one of you sick? He should call the elders of the church to pray over him and anoint him with oil in the name of the Lord. And the prayer offered in faith will make the sick person well; the Lord will raise him up. If he has sinned, he will be forgiven. Therefore confess your sins to each other and pray for each other so that you may be healed. The prayer of a righteous man is powerful and effective. (James 5:14-16)

Note: Share with your doctor any concerns you may have with the medical material given in chapters 8 through 12. Speak, also, to your pastor and the elders of your church about following the instructions given in James 5:14-16.

ELEVEN

How Positional Thinkers Deal with Social Damage

Finally, be strong in the Lord and in his mighty power. Put on the full armor of God so that you can take your stand against the devil's schemes. (Ephesians 6:10)

When we know that God accepts us, we accept ourselves even if the whole world rejects us. When we know experientially our acceptance and glorious freedom in Christ, we are set free from trying to please people. Then [when] others reject us (and they will), *they* have a problem![1]

—Charles R. Solomon

Positional Thinker's Action #11

"To overcome the social damage that comes from rejection and loneliness, I will not allow my sinful-nature thinking to convince me to isolate myself from others, but will be strong in the Lord and rest in God's acceptance of me."

There are six arrows that can damage relationships: loneliness, rejection, limited activities, family trauma, jealousy and cultural problems. Satan delights to invade our thought life during times of loneliness. Another weak spot is rejection, for when a patient is denied the love, care and acceptance he needs, he can be heartbroken. A life-threatening disease can traumatize the whole family. Our old sinful nature believes the disfigured or handicapped are objects of pity to be cast aside rather than precious souls whom God loves. This "old sinful nature" kind of thinking creeps so easily into the thought life.

How do we as positional thinkers battle this social warfare? We must take our seats in the heavenly realms where we are "strong in the Lord and in his mighty power. . . . Take your stand against the devil's schemes" (Ephesians 6:10-11). Remember that the devil is defeated. Think co-crucifixion, co-resurrection and co-seated. Make use of your weapons whenever one of these six social arrows tries to damage you. Here is your opportunity to stand on your positional sanctification and use your experiential sanctification in the social area. Don't forget that God's love in you is the greatest social remedy of all time!

Arrow Number Seven: Loneliness

Satan can use the fiery arrow of loneliness to make you despondent. He will use your disease to keep friends and family away. The partner without cancer often is afraid of "catching" the disease. Because of this, for example, a husband may experience secondary impotence after his wife is diagnosed with cervical cancer. Or a wife may become disinterested after her husband is diagnosed with bladder or prostate cancer. Even though people are repeatedly assured that cancer is not contagious, these irrational fears continue to contribute to sexual problems. Both partners need to offer continued warmth and reassurance throughout the low times. Staying physically close through touching and caressing helps to resume normal sexual relations when the sexual desire does return.

There is a certain amount of loneliness and anxiety when going through the testing and treatments at the hospital, as well as when you are home alone. There may be long periods of time during the day when your family and friends won't be present. Learn to fill up your time alone by reading good books. A reader never needs to stay lonely, because by reading you can get in touch with great minds and think their thoughts. This is a good opportunity to read the Bible and the book *Coping with Cancer: 12 Creative Choices*.

You may be gifted in handiwork or artistically inclined. I spent a good deal of time oil painting. Instead of being lonely, I chose to pick up the brushes and paint beautiful scenes on canvas. On blue skies I stroked bright sunshine that sent its warm rays past white puffy clouds to red and golden trees whose glorious colors were mirrored from peaceful lakes. With a song in my heart I would sing, "It is well, it is well with my soul." As I painted and sang, the thoughts of cancer and loneliness were replaced by creative thoughts of good things. This therapy assisted my body in the healing process.

PRAY THE FOLLOWING SCRIPTURE:

Above all, love each other deeply, because love covers over a multitude of sins. Offer hospitality to one another without grumbling. Each one should use whatever gift he has received to serve others, faithfully administering God's grace in its various forms. If anyone speaks, he should do it as one speaking the very words of God. If anyone serves, he should do it with the strength God provides, so that in all things God may be praised through Jesus Christ. To him be the glory and the power for ever and ever. Amen. (1 Peter 4:8-11)

Arrow Number Eight: Rejection

To reject a person is to deny that person the love, care and acceptance he needs. These qualities are especially needed when going through tough circumstances such as a life-threatening illness. Rejection is a difficult emotion to handle. You want acceptance from your peers. You desire to be on the inside track with them rather than the outside. You want acceptance of who you are with your own personality as well as your opinions, faults and recent illness. You don't relish a "put down" by people who try to change you to fit into their mold of acceptance.

But acceptance is not always forthcoming. Even Jesus was rejected by His own peers in His hometown after He announced He was going to preach the gospel. They didn't want Him inside their town. They drove Him out and tried to kill Him by throwing Him off the cliff. (Luke 4:16-30) This was the ultimate rejection —death!

How do you deal with the feeling of rejection? Are you indignant, embittered and nasty? Do you crawl into a shell and mope or laugh it off? Or do you share openly how badly you feel? This story about Jesus suggests four insights that you need to consider when coping with feelings of rejection.

1. God can give me the courage to do what's right despite criticism.
2. Rejection can help me examine my life and make the corrections needed.
3. Acceptance from my peers is not as important as God's love and acceptance of me.
4. Above all, think positionally to overcome the rejection in your social warfare. Note that Paul commands you to "[a]ccept one another . . . just as Christ accepted you" (Romans 15:7).

◆ **PRAY THE FOLLOWING SCRIPTURE:**

Each of us should please his neighbor for his good, to build him up. For even Christ did not please himself but, as it is written: "The insults of those who insult you have fallen on me." For everything that was written in the past was written to teach us, so that through endurance and the encouragement of the Scriptures we might have hope.

May the God who gives endurance and encouragement give you a spirit of unity among yourselves as you follow Christ Jesus, so that with one heart and mouth you may glorify the God and Father of our Lord Jesus Christ.

Accept one another, then, just as Christ accepted you, in order to bring praise to God. (Romans 15:2-7) ◆

Arrow Number Nine: Limited Activities

Limitation of activities is a reality Satan uses when a person is stricken with serious illness. Illness can upset well-established social patterns. Sports activities may be too strenuous. Entertaining is difficult when food doesn't taste good or when you are too tired to prepare a meal. Learn to put your own needs first and design social activities around those needs. Here are four ways people can customize their lives according to the *I Can Cope* program (which I have modified):

1. Learn to capitalize on what you have, not on what you have lost. If you enjoy jogging with another person, you may have to settle for walking instead. You may have to do it alone or with a person who enjoys walking. Start gradually and have your doctor approve anything unusual or strenuous.
2. Give yourself permission to indulge in what you enjoy. When you are feeling good, reward yourself without feeling guilty. If your favorite activity is traveling—indulge in that activity with your spouse or a friend when you are physically able.
3. Restructure your social environment based on your needs. Avoid people and places that make you feel uncomfortable or situations where you think others are uncomfortable around you. For many people, a support group is a great starting place.
4. Communicate! Make friends and loved ones aware of the duties you can or cannot manage right now. People who continue to do as much for themselves as possible usually feel better both physically, emotionally and socially. Don't allow others to treat you like an invalid if you don't feel like one. On the other

hand, if you are feeling tired or weak and want to be pampered, make sure that is understood also. Speak up for yourself.[2]

Limitation of social activities is often temporary and most people adapt well when loved ones are supportive.

PRAY THE FOLLOWING SCRIPTURE:

Praise the LORD, O my soul;
all my inmost being, praise his holy name.
Praise the LORD, O my soul,
and forget not all his benefits—
who forgives all your sins
and heals all your diseases,
who redeems your life from the pit
and crowns you with love and compassion,
who satisfies your desires with good things
so that your youth is renewed like the eagle's.
(Psalm 103:1-5)

Arrow Number Ten: Family Trauma

Sudden accidents and life-threatening disease can traumatize the whole family. Each member of the family, including the patient, may be on an emotional roller coaster ride. Tension and stress fill the air. Each day becomes a social threat and a spiritual battle. Individuals may react differently. Some may have resentments, while others may be very vocal or silent and withdrawn. Routines, responsibilities and relationships change. Beatrice Hoek writes:

> And often there isn't time to make the adjustments gradually; the family is rudely shoved into unfamiliar territory. Each day becomes an emotional challenge

> and spiritual battle, and each person struggles in different ways. At the very least, the family's cancer experience is unsettling. More often it is absolutely terrifying![3]

This is when prayer support of relatives, friends and churches will help relieve the tensions experienced by the family. A spouse needs to offer unrelenting support. You need to talk together and pray together. Express your stresses and conflicts.

◆ PRAY THE FOLLOWING SCRIPTURE:

> Be joyful always; pray continually; give thanks in all circumstances, for this is God's will for you in Christ Jesus.
>
> Do not put out the Spirit's fire; do not treat prophecies with contempt. Test everything. Hold on to the good. Avoid every kind of evil.
>
> May God himself, the God of peace, sanctify you through and through. May your whole spirit, soul and body be kept blameless at the coming of our Lord Jesus Christ. The one who calls you is faithful and he will do it. (1 Thessalonians 5:16-24) ◆

Arrow Number Eleven: Jealousy

Jealousy has been called "the green-eyed monster." It is Satan's tool to cause envy and resentment in a family setting. It is common, especially for young children, to feel intensively jealous of a sibling who has a serious illness. For example, a five-year-old brother has a six-year-old sister who is diagnosed with a heart problem. The sister needs to go to the hospital for treatments. The mother visits her often. She reads books and plays games with her.

When the mother isn't visiting, the sister watches cartoons on an unlimited basis. The brother believes this is a bit of heaven on earth. He becomes very jealous. A young child doesn't have the ability to see things from another child's perspective. He can't sympathize because he has never experienced the fear, weakness, nausea and pain that his sister feels.

How do you deal with jealousy? Be aware of this side effect. Know that children can't handle it properly. Let them talk about the disease from their perspective. Pray for guidance and try to explain the situation in their limited terminology.

◆ **PRAY THE FOLLOWING SCRIPTURE:**

> Love is patient, love is kind. It does not envy, it does not boast, it is not proud. It is not rude, it is not self-seeking, it is not easily angered, it keeps no record of wrongs. Love does not delight in evil but rejoices with the truth. It always protects, always trusts, always hopes, always perseveres.
>
> Love never fails. (1 Corinthians 13:4-8) ◆

Arrow Number Twelve: Cultural Problems

Every person has a cultural background. Culture defines what attire is acceptable, what attitudes should be toward the sick and dying, and how the aged and the disabled should be treated. Culture influences the behavior of others toward the sick person and the sick toward themselves. Cultural norms regulate whether someone can be among others or whether he will be isolated; also, whether the sick will be considered acceptable or whether they are to be pitied.

For example, a thirty-five-year-old sculptress found herself in a cultural predicament. Her illness began with breast cancer and soon spread to other areas of her body. She had extensive surgery and a regimen of medications to take. The medications caused her to become hairy and obese. Her face was changed by steroids. She was masculinized by her treatments and she had almost no hair. She lost the strength in her hand that she used for sculpturing. She fractured her femur which was delayed in being set while the physicians disagreed about pinning her hip. She was homebound and bed-bound. After a course of chemo, a new manifestation would appear. The nausea and vomiting were very distressing. She feared the future. Each tomorrow was seen as increased sickness, pain and disability.

What was the cultural problem? She felt isolated because of her disfigurement. She was no longer like other normal people accepted by her culture. The degree of importance attached to these losses caused her to suffer in relation to the world of events and relationships. She couldn't live in the world of her culture.

How can you cope with cultural problems? Our culture has been improving in the area of accepting the disfigured and the handicapped. The patients need their families and friends to accept and love them unconditionally. Churches need to look for these hurting people and offer a ministry of love and compassion. Share the gospel and the power of positional thinking with them.

PRAY THE FOLLOWING SCRIPTURE:

We know that the whole creation has been groaning as in the pains of childbirth right up to the present time. Not only so, but we ourselves, who have the firstfruits of the Spirit, groan inwardly as we wait eagerly for our adoption as sons, the redemption of our bodies. For in this hope we were saved. But hope that is seen is no hope at all. Who hopes for what he already has? But if we hope for what we do not yet have, we wait for it patiently. (Romans 8:22-25)

TWELVE

How Positional Thinkers Deal with Spiritual Damage

"For I know the plans I have for you," declares the L*ORD, "plans to prosper you and not to harm you, plans to give you hope and a future." (Jeremiah 29:11)*

A second key to mental and spiritual health . . . is to gradually learn to see our lives from God's perspective. As we do, we gain a whole new outlook on things and a much higher level of health. We are able to recognize the ultimate lie of Satan, that meaning to our lives comes by protecting ourselves, improving our position, and acquiring possessions. We learn the ultimate truth, that lasting security and significance come from submitting our lives to Christ, letting Him be our Lord.[1]

—Randy Reese and Frank Minirth

Positional Thinker's Action #12

"To overcome spiritual damage, I trust in the sovereignty of God to keep Satan from dimming my heavenly realms perspective by trying to keep me in the 'denial' and 'Why me, God?' mode."

Even though the devil is defeated, he still has his intimidating power. It is his unholy business to keep the believer from seeing the reigning Savior. Satan can cause spiritual damage through our sinful nature. We can experience shock and denial, the "Why me, God?" question, guilt, distance from God, a sense of insecurity and prayerlessness.

What are you to do? See your sanctification. Remember to trust in the sovereignty of God and let Christ be Lord of your life. Jesus has taken His seat of authority in the heavenlies. From this position He rules over the world, the sinful human nature and the devil. Since Jesus shares this authority with us, we are to exercise our positional thinking and use our weapons of warfare. The Word of God tells us that He has plans to give us a future and a hope. Hope is a powerful weapon. Let us also pray and use these weapons of hope and prayer to lessen the spiritual damage. We can rise above the tough circumstances with a victory that will bring glory to God!

Arrow Number Thirteen: Shock and Denial

Most people believe that life-threatening diseases such as heart disease or cancer will strike someone else, not them. It is not surprising that people respond to the diagnosis with shock and disbelief.

This was the same reaction that my wife and I experienced. The initial news of the diagnosis of cancer left Elaine and me in a temporary state of shock. She described the shock as being suddenly plunged into ice water and left numb with unbelief. Usually, family and friends are hit the same way. The patient and family try to find emotional relief by pretending this isn't happening, that it is a bad dream.

"I just can't believe this is happening to me." As the reality sets in, the patient will imagine exaggerated physical symptoms: the lump seems larger; the disease will spread; death is imminent. Denial distorts the reality of the disease.

Therefore, any attempt to avoid confronting the facts of the illness is harmful, especially in the long run. By allowing the denial to continue and refusing to discuss the disease openly, the family is actually making it harder for the patient to take the steps toward acceptance. There is a need to ventilate, no matter how difficult it is. You need to have spiritual support for all of the damaging arrows. Have a family member phone your pastor. Have your name placed on prayer chains in churches. Call for the elders of the church to pray and anoint with oil. Whether you, a family member or a friend is in a state of denial, be aware that a person needs time to work through this process. However, a lengthy stay in the denial stage is not healthy. Remember that the Word of God and prayer are the two most powerful spiritual weapons we have.

PRAY THIS SCRIPTURE FOR DAMAGE CONTROL:

By day the LORD directs his love,
  at night his song is with me—
  a prayer to the God of my life.

I say to God my Rock,
  "Why have you forgotten me?

Why must I go about mourning,
oppressed by the enemy?"
My bones suffer mortal agony
as my foes taunt me,
saying to me all day long,
"Where is your God?"

Why are you downcast, O my soul?
Why so disturbed within me?
Put your hope in God,
for I will yet praise him,
my Savior and my God.
(Psalm 42:8-11)

Arrow Number Fourteen: "Why Me, God?"

The second arrow is the "questioning God" arrow. Tormenting questions come very rapidly after the shocking diagnosis. Why me? What have I done? Is God punishing me? Is there anything I can do to find release? The very existence of suffering in a world created by an all-powerful, loving God has always perplexed thinking people. Even Christ came to suffer for us and with us. Jesus made it clear that we will suffer (see John 15:18-27).

The lesson I learned was not to dwell on the "why me" question when suddenly faced with a tough circumstance such as a life-threatening disease. It can only lead to discouragement, pity parties and depression. On this side of eternity it is difficult to understand the "why me" questions.

What should we do to solve this dilemma? We need to change the *why* to a *what* and trust in the sovereignty of God. "What do You want to teach me in this affliction in order that I may glorify You and grow spiritually?" "Help me to learn the lesson well so I won't need to go through it again." "I desire to be a good model that will bless others."

Jeremiah 29:11 states, " 'For I know the plans I have for you,' declares the LORD, 'plans to prosper you and not to harm you, plans to give you hope and a future.' " God permits adversity in His plan for you and me. He plans to prosper us spiritually, not to harm us. It is always the devil's plan to harm our spiritual lives.

PRAY THIS SCRIPTURE:

Trust in the LORD with all your heart
  and lean not on your own understanding;
in all your ways acknowledge him,
  and he will make your paths straight.

Do not be wise in your own eyes;
  fear the LORD and shun evil.
This will bring health to your body
  and nourishment to your bones.

Honor the LORD with your wealth,
  with the firstfruits of all your crops;
then your barns will be filled to overflowing,
  and your vats will brim over with new wine.

My son, do not despise the LORD's discipline
  and do not resent his rebuke,
because the LORD disciplines those he loves,
  as a father the son he delights in.
(Proverbs 3:5-12)

Arrow Number Fifteen: Guilt

Guilt feelings come when we condemn ourselves for violating a standard of right and wrong. We feel we have committed some sin and God is punishing us with an adversity. You may say, "I contracted this horrific disease because I wasn't living according to what I know to be right. I did something wrong. I have sinned. Thus, God is punishing me." This frame of mind would be termed "false guilt." Satan is delighted to use it to make us feel defeated.

All of us feel guilty from time to time. We are bombarded with lists of things we are supposed to do. When we don't keep our New Year's resolutions we feel guilty. Guilt is acceptable when we stray from the Lord or give in to temptation. This is true guilt. David had true guilt. He committed adultery and covered it up by committing murder. Later, he repented of his sin, as recorded in Psalm 51.

If you have true guilt over something you know you should not have done, admit it to the Lord Jesus, ask God's forgiveness and repent. For example if you are a cigarette smoker and have lung cancer or emphysema, confess and ask forgiveness from God. Then give up smoking. Identify with the people of God. Build close relationships to those who can "spur one another on toward love and good deeds" (Hebrews 10:24).

PRAY THE FOLLOWING SCRIPTURE:

> Have mercy on me, O God,
> according to your unfailing love;
> according to your great compassion
> blot out my transgressions.
> Wash away all my iniquity
> and cleanse me from my sin.
>
> For I know my transgressions,
> and my sin is always before me.
> Against you, you only, have I sinned

and done what is evil in your sight,
so that you are proved right when you speak
and justified when you judge. . . .

Let me hear joy and gladness;
let the bones you have crushed rejoice.
Hide your face from my sins
and blot out all my iniquity.

Create in me a pure heart, O God,
and renew a steadfast spirit within me.
(Psalm 51:1-4, 8-10) ◆

Arrow Number Sixteen: God Seems Far Away

What can we do when God appears to be far away, when it seems He has abandoned us at a time when we need Him the most? What can we do when our prayers seem to reach no higher than the ceiling? We need to realize that what seems to be and what is true reality are not the same.

In the story of Job in the Old Testament, Job cried out to God, but He didn't answer him. Job said, "If I go to the north, east, south or west, I don't find him" (Job 23:8-9, author paraphrase). Despite his lack of discovery, however, Job still held on to his faith. Later, he wrote, "But he knows the way that I take; when he has tested me, I will come forth as gold" (23:10). In saying this, Job recognized the omnipresence of God. Though Job did not hear Him, see Him or sense His presence, he still believed that God was right there with him. His silence during our greatest need is meant to test us. This leads us to a greater, stronger faith.

◆ **PRAY THE FOLLOWING SCRIPTURE:**

Where can I go from your Spirit?
  Where can I flee from your presence?
If I go up to the heavens, you are there;
  if I make my bed in the depths, you are there.
If I rise on the wings of the dawn,
  if I settle on the far side of the sea,
even there your hand will guide me,
  your right hand will hold me fast.

If I say, "Surely the darkness will hide me
  and the light become night around me,"
even the darkness will not be dark to you;
  the night will shine like the day,
  for darkness is as light to you.
(Psalm 139:7-12) ◆

Arrow Number Seventeen: Insecurity

Satan tries to impose on us the feeling of insecurity. We feel like all the props have been kicked out from under us. It is like being separated from your company in battle, cut off from security and any hope of defeating the enemy. We need to replace this destructive thinking with the positive Word of God given to believers in Romans 8:35-39. In this passage our security is guaranteed by God's love. The major emphasis is that nothing shall separate us from God's love, not even the most extreme adversities in life.

The reassuring, exciting part of this passage are the words: "[I]n all these things we are more than conquerors" (8:37). Our conquest is more than merely winning a victory; it is gaining a special advantage over Satan, who has already been conquered. In overcoming the foe we learn lessons that could never have been learned in any other way. Each trouble, hardship or persecution is a test that can make us more than conquerors over our tough circumstances. This is using adversity to our advantage so that something that Satan plans for evil may turn out for our spiritual good.

PRAY THE FOLLOWING SCRIPTURE:

> Who shall separate us from the love of Christ? Shall trouble or hardship or persecution or famine or nakedness or danger or sword? As it is written:
>
> "For your sake we face death all day long;
> we are considered as sheep to be slaughtered."
>
> No, in all these things we are more than conquerors through him who loved us. For I am convinced that neither death nor life, neither angels nor demons, neither the present nor the future, nor any powers, neither height nor depth, nor anything else in all creation, will be able to separate us from the love of God that is in Christ Jesus our Lord. (Romans 8:35-39)

Arrow Number Eighteen: Prayerlessness

We can allow ourselves to become so disillusioned with our illness that we stop praying altogether. If we find ourselves in this rut we need to replace the negative, destructive disillusionment with the positive, healing Word of God. Our selections for praying the Scriptures are Romans 8:26-28 and Hebrews 4:14-16. In these verses, we see that a Christian is not left in unpleasant circumstances without a helper; "the Spirit helps us in our weakness" (Romans 8:26). In our helplessness we cannot even pray as we ought to pray; but in the midst of it all, God gives us this wonderful assurance; the Spirit helps us in our weakness. He takes our groaning, those longings within for which we are trying to find words of expression, and interprets them correctly, presenting our deepest desires to God on our behalf. He prays for us! And when the Holy Spirit intercedes for us, He does it, "in accordance with God's will" (8:27).

Remember Jesus is our great high priest who is able "to sympathize with our weaknesses" (Hebrews 4:15) because He was clothed with our humanity, yet without sin. He has compassion and understands all our perplexities. Theodore Epp wrote the following:

> Whether we can express our needs and desires in words or not, the Spirit of God helps us before the throne. So we have a faithful Father who cares for us, a High Priest who faithfully prays for us and the Holy Spirit faithfully praying within us. . . . All three members of the Godhead stand ready to help us. Thus we can approach His throne of grace only because of our position in Christ.[2]

Practice your positional thinking. All three members of the Godhead are ready to help us in the good fight of faith.

PRAY THE FOLLOWING SCRIPTURE:

> In the same way, the Spirit helps us in our weakness. We do not know what we ought to pray for, but the Spirit himself intercedes for us with groans that words cannot express. And he who searches our hearts knows the mind of the Spirit, because the Spirit intercedes for the saints in accordance with God's will.

And we know that in all things God works for the good of those who love him, who have been called according to his purpose. (8:26-28)

Therefore, since we have a great high priest who has gone through the heavens, Jesus the Son of God, let us hold firmly to the faith we profess. For we do not have a high priest who is unable to sympathize with our weaknesses, but we have one who has been tempted in every way, just as we are—yet was without sin. Let us then approach the throne of grace with confidence, so that we may receive mercy and find grace to help us in our time of need. (Hebrews 4:14-16) ◆

THIRTEEN

How Positional Thinkers Deal with Psychological Damage

Do not get drunk on wine, which leads to debauchery. Instead, be filled with the Spirit. (Ephesians 5:18)

Total counseling takes seriously the commandment to be "filled with the Spirit" (Ephesians 5:18). In the context, the phrase is set over against a life-dominating sin: drunkenness ("Do not get drunk with wine . . . but be filled with the Spirit"). As that which must replace such sins, the apostle commands, "be filled with" (let your life be dominated and controlled by) the Spirit. To be "filled with" fear, or joy, or sorrow in the Scriptures means to be so affected by these that they dominate and control all of one's life.[1]

—Jay E. Adams

Positional Thinker's Action #13

"To overcome bitterness, poor personal worth, depression, anxiety, fear of the future and death, and loss of control, I will trust the Holy Spirit to fill and control me."

Let us not have the impression that spiritual warfare and psychology are the same. Satan, however, carries spiritual warfare to the psychological area. Our arch foe is shrewdly at work trying to damage us psychologically through bitterness, poor personal worth, depression, fear of the future and death, anxiety, worry and loss of control. Our struggle in this psychological area is with our old nature trying to take the upper hand over our new nature.

By now you should be in the habit of using your spiritual authority and feeling at home in your seat in the heavenly realms. Count yourself dead to sin and alive to God in Christ Jesus. Satan wants you to remain depressed and bitter. Don't give him that satisfaction! Remember that Christ's victory over Satan is your victory. Experience sanctification! Think co-crucifixion, co-resurrection and being co-seated with Christ. Take your weapons of praise, faith, hope, love, God's Word and prayer to dispel any psychological damage that may occur.

This chapter explains briefly the characteristics of these psychological areas. Positional thinking will assist you, along with the scriptural instructions given, as you work through each one. Remember this truth: the love of God is the foundation for dealing with all psychological problems we face in our tough circumstances. Be determined not to be dominated by sinful-nature thinking, but be dominated and controlled by the Holy Spirit, which is new-nature thinking.

Arrow Number Nineteen: Bitterness

Bitterness comes from our own personal reaction to irritations and problems in life. We must recognize that people or illnesses don't make us bitter or resentful, regardless of what they do to us. It is our issue because we have wrongfully responded to the problems and irritations of life. Our sinful nature places the blame on others, but we must take the responsibility for our own personal reactions.

Paul wrote, "See to it that no one misses the grace of God and that no bitter root grows up to cause trouble and defile many" (Hebrews 12:15). The phrase "grows up" in the Greek means "to sprout up quickly." It is a quick process. The word "defile" means "to dye or stain." Put a drop of black ink in a glass of water and it will discolor the whole glass of water. In the same way, bitterness works quickly to hurt everyone involved in trying to help the patient.

Our resentments call forth certain hormones from the pituitary, adrenal, thyroid and other glands. Excessive hormones can cause disease in any part of the body to complicate the healing process. Major hindrances to spiritual development take place. It requires emotional energy to maintain resentment. The moment I start resenting a person, serious mental consequences occur. I become his slave because he controls my thoughts. When I'm served steak and potatoes it might as well be bread and water. Solomon wrote, "Better a meal of vegetables where there is love than a fattened calf with hatred" (Proverbs 15:17).

Bitterness can be healed by forgiveness. If Jesus forgave us, with all our offenses, we ought to forgive one another.

Forgiving persons is clearing their record with us. It is made possible through the cross. Jesus didn't become bitter toward those who beat Him and nailed Him to the cross. He prayed in their hearing, "Father, forgive them; for they know not what they do" (Luke 23:34, KJV).

Replace resentment and bitterness with kindness and forgiveness. By doing it God's way, you will hasten the healing process.

PRAY THIS SCRIPTURE:

Your righteousness reaches to the skies, O God,
you who have done great things.
Who, O God, is like you?
Though you have made me see troubles,
many and bitter,
you will restore my life again;
from the depths of the earth
you will again bring me up.
You will increase my honor
and comfort me once again. . . .

My lips will shout for joy
when I sing praise to you—
I, whom you have redeemed.
(Psalm 71:19-21, 23)

Get rid of all bitterness, rage and anger, brawling and slander, along with every form of malice. Be kind and compassionate to one another, forgiving each other, just as in Christ God forgave you. (Ephesians 4:31-32)

Arrow Number Twenty: Poor Personal Worth

Bad circumstances with chronic and life-threatening diseases can produce feelings of worthlessness within us. Personal worth is determined by a person's evaluation of himself. It is a universal built-in problem that comes from our original sin. It says, "I'm not OK. Others may be, but I'm not." This self-doubt affects some people more than others, depending on whether or not you suffered nonaccepting, nonapproving relationships in growing up. If we have these negative relationships with the important people in our lives, we get the impression, "I'm not valuable." Then when such a person contracts a serious illness, is involved in a serious auto accident or is burned terribly, it merely validates their worthlessness.

What is the scriptural solution to the dilemma of poor personal worth? We must not evaluate ourselves on the disapproval of others, but on God's evaluation of us. Paul gave us sound advice on building personal identity. He said, "For by the grace given me I say to every one of you: Do not think of yourself more highly than you ought, but rather think of yourself with sober judgment, in accordance with the measure of faith God has given you" (Romans 12:3). He goes on in the context to discuss spiritual gifts. Each believer is so valuable a member of the body of Christ that each person is given at least one spiritual gift to fulfill his role. These ministries are given as a gift of grace and not given according to our performance. Our personal worth is based on God and what He has done for us and given to us, not on comparing ourselves with others.

Calvary demonstrates once and for all that we are not worthless. God loves us and Christ died for us. Our goal is to become like Christ (8:29). We are to love the Lord and love our neighbors as ourselves (Luke 10:27). When we are convinced that we are valuable in God's eyes, we are free to reach out in love to others, even in tough circumstances.

PRAY THIS SCRIPTURE:

> Are not two sparrows sold for a penny? Yet not one of them will fall to the ground apart from the will of your Father. And even the very hairs of your head are all numbered. So don't be afraid; you are worth more than many sparrows. (Matthew 10:29-31)
>
> How great is the love the Father has lavished on us, that we should be called children of God! And that is what we are! The reason the world does not know us is that it did not know him. Dear friends, now we are children of God, and what we will be has not yet been made known. But we know that when he appears, we shall be like him, for we shall see him as he is. Everyone who has this hope in him purifies himself, just as he is pure. (1 John 3:1-3)

Arrow Twenty-One: Depression

One of the most effective fiery arrows that Satan uses in debilitating the Christian in tough circumstances is depression. Psychologists believe that it causes much human suffering. Depression has at least four main causes.

1. Depression is the result of not handling our life God's way. Jonah should have rejoiced when Nineveh repented (Jonah 3:10-4:3), which was God's way, but instead he allowed himself to become depressed. His inward hostility toward the Ninevites turned into anger. We may not be responsible for the problems of life, but we are responsible for the way we respond to and handle these problems.

2. Depression is caused by self-pity. When Elijah thought he was alone in his battle against Jezebel, he indulged in self-pity which led to depression. Self-pity is dealing with life's problems from a self-centered point of view. God reminded him that there were 7,000 men in Israel who had never bowed to Baal. God also urged Elijah to get into action to counteract his problem. He gave Elijah the realistic hope he could do something about his depression. And Elijah did, with God's help. So can we!
3. Depression is caused by one's mental attitude toward the circumstances of life. Moses became depressed several times as he led the Israelites in the wilderness. Note how he reveals his feeling of depression: "If this is how you are going to treat me, put me to death right now—if I have found favor in your eyes—and do not let me face my own ruin" (Numbers 11:15). Moses lost hope. He'd rather have died than to have put forth any more effort. He lost his perspective. He wanted to escape from his circumstance.

   Depression must be dealt with in the light of the cross. The only way to stand up against it is to recognize it as sin, repent of it and ask the Holy Spirit to fill you. When the Christian is filled with the Holy Spirit, no room exists for depression!
4. The fourth cause of depression can be the effects of medication. If this is your case, let your doctor know.

Pray for comfort and endurance for all four causes of depression.

◆ **PRAY THIS PASSAGE OF SCRIPTURE:**

Praise be to the God and Father of our Lord Jesus Christ, the Father of compassion and the God of all

> comfort, who comforts us in all our troubles, so that we can comfort those in any trouble with the comfort we ourselves have received from God. For just as the sufferings of Christ flow over into our lives, so also through Christ our comfort overflows. If we are distressed, it is for your comfort and salvation; if we are comforted, it is for your comfort, which produces in you patient endurance of the same sufferings we suffer. And our hope for you is firm, because we know that just as you share in our sufferings, so also you share in our comfort. (2 Corinthians 1:3-7)

Arrow Twenty-Two: Fear of the Future and Death

Life-threatening diseases bring a person face-to-face with the possibility of death. Five psychological stages, when facing death, have been made famous by Dr. Elizabeth Kubler-Ross. They are 1) shock, 2) denial, 3) bargaining with God, 4)depression and 5) acceptance.[2]

They strike us with tremendous impact! Understanding these stages helps us to work through them. If a loved one is experiencing their impact, we can, with patience and compassion, help them. The psalmist pictures life-threatening circumstances as a dark valley (Psalm 23:4). The New Testament states that death is an enemy. One day that enemy will be destroyed (1 Corinthians 15:26).

We may fear a long lingering, painful suffering that precedes death more than we fear death itself. We need to recognize, however, that great discoveries have been made in the field of pain control. Persons are able to receive relief from pain when they make their wishes known. The fear of a long terminal sickness also raises other fears such as the fear of being a burden to loved ones, the fear of impairment and being unable to care for oneself, and even fears associated with the high cost of health care.

How can we be helpful to friends or loved ones? Let me mention five ways: 1) Be truthful—never belittle the circumstance; 2) be a good listener—let a person talk out their feelings through each stage; 3) reach out to help and enlist the help of others to keep the pet, water plants, mow the lawn, etc.; 4) always offer hope—have something the person can look forward to; 5) offer spiritual support and share comforting passages of Scripture, such as those referring to heaven. Pray together. Give him a copy of this book or read it to him.

PRAY THIS SCRIPTURE:

The LORD is my shepherd, I shall not be in want.
He makes me lie down in green pastures,
he leads me beside quiet waters,
he restores my soul.
He guides me in paths of righteousness
for his name's sake.
Even though I walk
through the valley of the shadow of death,
I will fear no evil,
for you are with me;
your rod and your staff,
they comfort me.

You prepare a table before me
in the presence of my enemies.
You anoint my head with oil;
my cup overflows.

Surely goodness and love will follow me
all the days of my life,
and I will dwell in the house of the LORD
forever. (Psalm 23)

Arrow Twenty-Three: Anxiety and Worry

Many psychologists believe that anxiety is the root of many psychological disorders. The anxious person is torn apart emotionally. That is the basic meaning of the word. Thus, anxiety and worry are very destructive and are used by the devil to disturb the peace of God in the life of the believer.

Jesus taught that anxiety and worry must stop controlling the believer's life. He said, "Do not worry" three times in Matthew 6:25-34. He concluded, "Each day has enough trouble of its own" (6:34). We are to live one day at a time in a trusting relationship. Anxiety and worry about the future are useless and achieve nothing. Why let tomorrow's problems tear you apart today?

Let us look at three people of faith who could have worried about their difficult circumstance but didn't. Abraham was told to go out of his country. He didn't worry about where he was going to reside permanently. Joseph, while in prison, could have worried that God had forgotten him and whether his dreams would come true. Esther could have worried so much about whether she would be executed for going in to see the king that she never would have gone.

Paul, in Philippians 4:4-7, was in prison as he penned these words, "Do not be anxious about anything." He was echoing the admonition of Jesus. Then he offers a fourfold biblical solution: 1) rejoice; 2) the Lord is near; 3) pray and 4) give thanksgiving. What is the result? The peace of God will guard both our hearts and our minds from the damage that Satan's arrows of anxiety and worry tries to inflict.

PRAY THIS SCRIPTURE:

> Rejoice in the Lord always. I will say it again: Rejoice! Let your gentleness be evident to all. The Lord is near. Do not be anxious about anything, but in everything, by prayer and petition, with thanksgiving, present your requests to God. And the peace of God, which transcends all understanding, will guard your hearts and your minds in Christ Jesus. (Philippians 4:4-7)

Arrow Twenty-Four: Loss of Control

Loss of control is a fiery arrow used by Satan to render us emotionally fearful. Life-threatening diseases convey very intimidating, controlling thoughts. We think, "Don't diseases control the body? Doesn't the medical team control the treatment? Doesn't the disease also control our thinking?" The logical follow-up question is, "What is left for the patient to control?" There are activities you can control. For example, you can control your relationship with God, your relationship with people, your goal setting and your diet. You need, also, to have control in decisions related to medical treatment.

I have found out from experience that we need to replace the loss of control with the control of God. An example of alcoholism in Ephesians 5:18 gives us insight in what the loss of control does to us. It's interesting that the Bible uses the analogy of drunkenness to teach us how

God wants to control us. Paul declares, "Be not drunk with wine . . . but be filled with the Spirit" (KJV). The alcohol controls how a person walks, talks, sees and thinks. Likewise, being filled with the Holy Spirit means that every thought, word and action is brought under God's control.

How can we describe this control? We can take an iron bar and place it into fire. We have two substances—fire and iron. Soon the fire is in the iron, just as the iron in the fire. Thus, the Holy Spirit penetrates the spirit of a person. In the whole experience we remain ourselves. It is only when filled with the Spirit that our personality is fully realized. We will never know the full possibilities of our redeemed personalities until we yield completely to His control.

PRAY THIS SCRIPTURE:

> Have I not commanded you? Be strong and courageous. Do not be terrified; do not be discouraged, for the LORD your God will be with you wherever you go. (Joshua 1:9)
>
> Be very careful, then, how you live—not as unwise but as wise, making the most of every opportunity, because the days are evil. Therefore do not be foolish, but understand what the Lord's will is. Do not get drunk on wine, which leads to debauchery. Instead, be filled with the Spirit. Speak to one another with psalms, hymns and spiritual songs. Sing and make music in your heart to the Lord, always giving thanks to God the Father for everything, in the name of our Lord Jesus Christ. (Ephesians 5:15-20)

Conclusion

It has been my intention to have a balanced and sane approach to the subject of spiritual warfare as it relates to persons who are battling chronic and life-threatening diseases or other tough circumstances. We must be careful not to see a demon under every bush. Likewise, must not blame the devil for all our actions and say, "The devil made me do it," thereby excusing our personal responsibility for sin.

If you have not been taking personal responsibility for your sinful nature, I would encourage you to reread chapter 2. Concentrate prayerfully on "The ABCs to Receive Justification and Spiritual Healing." If you haven't received Christ Jesus into your life, receive Him without delay. Repeat the sample prayer and sign the consent form. Begin to practice your authoritative position in Christ over the forces of evil.

Let us not be overly preoccupied with Satan. Let us, instead, be preoccupied with God the Father, God the Son and God the Holy Spirit. The enormous power of God that raised Jesus from the dead and seated Him at the right hand of God in the heavenly realm is available to us who believe. Jesus has broken the power of Satan and our old sinful nature and has raised us to an authoritative position of positive strength and assurance. Think co-crucifixion, co-resurrection and being co-seated with Christ when Satan tries to damage you physically, socially, spiritually or psychologically. Meditate on the "Positional Thinker's Action Cards" and you will win over your tough circumstances with joyful victory!

Notes

Chapter 1 Positional Power Brings Authority to the Believer

1. Keith Bailey, *Strange Gods* (Camp Hill, PA: Christian Publications, 1998), p. 212.

2. K. Neill Foster, *Warfare Weapons* (Camp Hill, PA: Christian Publications, 1995), p. 116.

3. Ed Murphy, *The Handbook for Spiritual Warfare* (Nashville TN: Thomas Nelson, n.d.), p. 393.

4. John A. MacMillan, *The Authority of the Believer* (Camp Hill, PA: Christian Publications, 1980), p. 41.

Chapter 2 How Positional Thinking Differs from Positive Thinking

1. Harold M. Freligh, *The Eight Pillars of Salvation* (Minneapolis, MN: Bethany Fellowship, 1947), p. 69.

2. H. Norman Wright, *Self-Talk, Imagery, and Prayer in Counseling*, vol. 3 (Waco, TX: Word Books, 1985), p. 59.

3. F. Minirth et al., *The Healthy Christian Life* (Grand Rapids, MI: Baker Book House, 1988), p. 139.

4. Roy C. Putnam, *In It to Win It* (Fort Washington, PA: Christian Literature Crusade, 1993), pp. 111-112.

5. John E. Packo, *Coping with Cancer: 12 Creative Choices* (Camp Hill, PA: Christian Publications, 1991), p. 120.

Chapter 3 Think Co-Crucifixion

1. J. Gregory Mantle, *Keswick's Authentic Voice* (Grand Rapids, MI: Zondervan, 1959), p. 340.

Chapter4 Think Co-Resurrection

1. Putnam, p. 105.

2. A.B. Simpson, *Romans* (Harrisburg, PA: Christian Publications, n.d.), p. 139.

3. Don J. Kenyon, *Romans,* vol. 1 (Harrisburg, PA: Christian Publications, 1978), p. 16.

4. George Pardington, "The Law of Reckoning," *Alliance Life*, November 9, 1988, p. 9.

5. Putnam, p. 107.

6. John F. Walvoord, *Major Bible Prophecies* (Grand Rapids, MI: Zondervan, 1991), p. 27.

7. Ibid., p. 28.

8. McCandlish Phillips, *The Spirit World* (Wheaton, IL: Victor Books, 1973), p. 92.

Chapter 5 Think Co-Seated

1. Watchman Nee, *Sit Walk Stand* (Fort Washington, PA: Christian Literature Crusade, 1958), p. 5.

2. John F. Walvoord, *Major Bible Prophecies* (Grand Rapids, MI: Zondervan, 1991), p. 428.

Chapter 6 Test the Spirits

1. Kurt Koch, *Demonology Past and Present* (Grand Rapids, MI: Kregel Publications, 1973), p. 140.

2. Neil T. Anderson, *The Bondage Breaker* (Eugene, OR: Harvest House, 1990), p. 235.

3. Elio Cuccaro, ed. *Alliance Academic Review* (1997) (Camp Hill, PA: Christian Publications, 1997), p. 167.

4. Ibid.

Chapter 7 Four Powerful Weapons to Defeat Destructive Thinking

1. A.W. Tozer, *Whatever Happened to Worship?* (Camp Hill, PA: Christian Publications, 1985), p. 24.

2. Foster, p. 30.

3. Ibid., p. 31.

4. Warren Wiersbe, *Real Worship* (Nashville, TN: Oliver Nelson, 1986), p. 29.

5. Charles B. Clayman, *Home Medical Encyclopedia* (New York: Random House, 1989), p. 351.

6. Foster, pp. 155, 161.

Chapter 8 Two Offensive Weapons to Defeat Destructive Thinking

1. Foster, p. 20.

Chapter 9 Practicing Positional Thinking in Tough Circumstances

1. Miles J. Stanford, *The Complete Green Letters* (Grand Rapids, MI: Zondervan, 1983), p. 257.

2. Taken from the chapter "The Power of Positional Thinking" from my book *Coping with Cancer* (published by Christian Publications).

Chapter 10 How Positional Thinkers Deal with Physical Damage

1. Robert G. Witty, *Divine Healing* (Nashville, TN: Broadman Press, 1989) p. 155.

2. Judi Johnson and Linda Klein, *I Can Cope* (Minneapolis, MN: DCI Publishing, 1988), p. 82.

3. Bruce B. Miller, *The Immune System: Nutrition for Optimal Wellness* (Dallas, TX: Bruce Miller Enterprises, Inc., 1989), p. 4.

4. The Associated Press, "Duke Study Connects Health with Church Attendance," *Asheville Citizen-Times*, October 23, 1997, n.p.

5. Matthew Hoffman and William LeGro, *Disease Free: How to Prevent, Treat, and Cure More Than 150 Illnesses and Conditions* (Emmaus, PA: Berkley Publishing Group, 1993), p. 282.

Chapter 11 How Positional Thinkers Deal with Social Damage

1. Charles Solomon, *The Ins and Outs of Rejection* (Littleton, CO: Heritage House Publications, 1976), p. 55.

2. Johnson and Klein, p. 94.

3. Beatrice H. Hoek, *Cancer Lives at Our House: Help for the Family* (Grand Rapids, MI: Baker Books, 1997), p. 40.

Chapter 12 How Positional Thinkers Deal with Spiritual Damage

1. Randy Reese and Frank Minirth, *Growing Into Wholeness* (Chicago, IL: Moody Press, 1993), p. 111.

2. Theodore H. Epp, *Victory Triumphant and Practical*, vol. 3 (Lincoln, NE: Back to the Bible Publishers, 1959), p. 45.

Chapter 13 How Positional Thinkers Deal with Psychological Damage

1. Jay Adams, *The Christian Counselor's Manual* (Grand Rapids, MI: Baker Book House, 1973), p. 208.

2. Elizabeth Kubler-Ross, *On Death and Dying* (New York: Collier Books, 1997), chapters 1-4.

BIBLIOGRAPHY

Adams, Jay E. *The Christian Counselor's Manual*. Grand Rapids, MI: Baker Book House, 1973.

Anderson, Neil T. *Living Free in Christ*. Ventura, CA: Regal Books, 1993.

———. *Winning Spiritual Warfare*. Eugene, OR: Harvest House Publishers, 1990.

———. *The Bondage Breaker*. Eugene, OR: Harvest House Publishers, 1990.

Backus, William. *The Healing Power of a Healthy Mind*. Minneapolis, MN: Bethany House Publishers, 1996.

Bailey, Keith M. *The Children's Bread*. Camp Hill, PA: Christian Publications, 1977.

———. *Strange Gods*. Camp Hill, PA: Christian Publications, 1998.

Baker, Don. *Acceptance*. Portland, OR: Multnomah Press, 1985.

Barnes, Albert. *Barnes' Notes on the New Testament*. Grand Rapids, MI: Kregel Publications, 1962.

Bayly, Joseph. *The View from a Hearse*. Colorado Springs, CO: David C. Cook, 1969.

Billheimer, Paul E. *Don't Waste Your Sorrows*. Minneapolis, MN: Bethany House Publishers, 1977.

Boettner, Loraine. *Studies in Theology*. Grand Rapids, MI: Eerdmans, 1951.

Boles, Richard N. *The Three Boxes of Life*. Berkley, CA: Ten Speed Press, 1981.

Cherry, Reginald. *The Bible Cure*. Orlando, FL: Creation House, 1998.

Clayman, Charles B. *Home Medical Encyclopedia*. New York: Random House, 1989.

Collins, Gary R. *Christian Counseling*. Waco, TX: Word Books, 1980.

Cornwall, Judson. *Praying the Scriptures*. Lake Mary, FL: Creation House, 1982.

Cuccaro, Elio. *Alliance Academic Review* (1997). Camp Hill, PA: Christian Publications, 1997.

Detzler, Wayne A. *New Testament Words in Today's Language*. Wheaton, IL: Victor Books, 1986.

Duewel, Wesley L. *Touch the World Through Prayer*. Grand Rapids, MI: Zondervan, 1986.

"Duke Study Connects Health with Church Attendance," *Ashville Citizen-Times*, October 23, 1997.

Epp, Theodore H. *Victory Triumphant and Practical*. Lincoln, NE: Back to the Bible Publishers, 1959.

Fintel, William A. and Gerald R. McDermott. *A Medical and Spiritual Guide to Living with Cancer*. Dallas TX: Word Publishing, 1993.

Foster, K. Neill. *Binding and Loosing*. Camp Hill, PA: Christian Publications, 1998.

———. *Warfare Weapons*. Camp Hill, PA: Christian Publications, 1995.

Freligh, Harold M. *The Eight Pillars of Salvation*. Minneapolis: Bethany Fellowship, Inc., 1964.

———. *Job—An Early Document of Fundamental Doctrines*. Harrisburg, PA: Christian Publications, 1947.

Fry, William. "Have a Hearty Laugh." *Ladies Home Journal*, November 1994.

Harrison, Everett F. *Baker's Dictionary of Theology*. Grand Rapids, MI: Baker Book House, 1960.

Hoek, Beatrice H. and Melanie Jongsma. *Cancer Lives at Our House, Help for the Family*. Grand Rapids, MI: Baker Book House, 1997.

Hoffman, Matthew and William Legro. *Disease Free*. Emmaus, PA: Rodale Press, 1993.

Johnson, Arthur. *Battle for World Evangelism*. Wheaton, IL: Tyndale House Publishers, 1978.

Johnson, Judi and Linda Klein. *I Can Cope*. Minneapolis, MN: DCI Publishing, 1988.

Kenyon, Don J. *Romans vol. 1*. Harrisburg, PA: Christian Publications, 1978.

Koch, Kurt. *Demonology Past and Present*. Grand Rapids, MI: Kregel Publications, 1973.

Kubler-Ross, Elizabeth. *On Death and Dying*. New York: Collier Books, 1997.

MacMillan, John A. *The Authority of the Believer*. Camp Hill, PA: Christian Publications, 1980.

Mantle, J. Gregory, *Keswick's Authentic Voice*. Grand Rapids, MI: Zondervan, 1959.

Miller, Bruce B. *The Immune System: Nutrition for Optimal Wellness*. Dallas, TX: Bruce Miller Enterprises, Inc, 1989.

Minirth F., et al. *The Healthy Christian Life*. Grand Rapids, MI: Zondervan, 1988.

Murphy, Ed. *The Handbook for Spiritual Warfare*. Nashville TN: Thomas Nelson, 1992.

Narramore, Clyde M. *The Psychology of Counseling*. Grand Rapids, MI: Zondervan, 1978.

Nee, Watchman. *Sit Walk Stand*. Fort Washington, PA: Christian Literature Crusade, 1958.

Neff, Lavonne, et al. *Practical Christianity*. Wheaton, IL: Tyndale House Publishers, 1978.

Newell, William R. *Romans*. Chicago, IL: Moody Press, 1938.

Ogilvie, Lloyd J. *Conversation with God*. Eugene, OR: Harvest House, 1993.

———. *Making Stress Work for You*. Waco, TX: Word Books, 1985.

Packo, John E. *Coping with Cancer: 12 Creative Choices*. Camp Hill, PA: Christian Publications, 1991.

———. *Find and Use Your Spiritual Gifts*. Camp Hill, PA: Christian Publications, 1980.

Pardington, George. "The Law of Reckoning," *The Alliance Life*, November 9, 1988.

Petersen, J. Allen. *ReACT—You Are Really Somebody!* Wheaton IL: Family Concern, 1979.

Phillips, McCandlish. *The Spirit World*. Wheaton, IL: Victor Books, 1973.

Pierson, Arthur T. *In Christ Jesus*. Chicago: Moody Press, 1974.

Putnam, Roy C. *In It to Win It*. Fort Washington, PA: Christian Literature Crusade, 1993.

Richards, Lawrence O. *The Believer's Guidebook*. Grand Rapids, MI: Zondervan, 1983.

Reese, Randy and Frank Minirth. *Growing into Wholeness*. Chicago, IL: Moody Press, 1993.

Schmidt, Jerry A. *Do You Hear What You're Thinking?*. Wheaton, IL: Victor Books, 1989.

Seamands, David A. *Healing Grace*. Wheaton, IL: Victor Books, 1988.

Simpson, A.B. *Romans*, vol. 17. Harrisburg, PA: Christian Publications, n.d.

Solomon, Charles. *The Ins and Out of Rejection*. Littleton, CO: Heritage House Publications, 1976.

Stanford, Miles J. *The Complete Green Letters*. Grand Rapids: Zondervan, 1983.

Tozer, A.W. *How to Try the Spirits*. Camp Hill, PA: Christian Publications, 1997.

———. *Whatever Happened to Worship?* Camp Hill, PA: Christian Publications, 1997.

Veith, Gene E. "Christ and Culture." *WORLD*, May 23, 1998.

Walvoord, John E. *Major Bible Prophecies*. Grand Rapids, MI: Zondervan, 1991.

———. *Prophecy Knowledge Handbook*. Wheaton, IL: Victor Books, 1990.

Wiersbe, Warren. *Real Worship*. Nashville, TN: Oliver Nelson, 1986.

Witty, Robert G. *Divine Healing*. Nashville, TN: Broadman Press, 1989.

White, Tom. "Is This Really Warfare?" *Discipleship Journal*, May/June, 1994.

Wright, H. Norman. *Self-Talk, Imagery, and Prayer in Counseling*, vol. 3. Waco, TX: Word Books, 1985.

Zacharias, Ravi. *Deliver Us from Evil*. Dallas, TX: Word Publishing, 1996.

Subject Index

A

B

C

D

E

F

G

H

I

J

K

L

M

N

O

P

R

S

T

U

W

Scripture Index

Genesis

Numbers

Joshua

First Kings

Second Kings

Job

Psalms

Proverbs

Jeremiah

Jonah

Matthew

Mark

Luke

John

Romans

First Corinthians

Second Corinthians

Galatians

Ephesians

Philippians

Colossians

First Thessalonians

Second Thessalonians

First Timothy

Second Timothy

Titus

Hebrews

James

First Peter

First John

Revelation

Positional Thinker's Action #1

"I use the authority, delegated to me by Christ, which is as powerful as the power that raised Jesus from the dead and seated Him at God's right hand in the heavenly realms. This action defeated Satan, his demons, the world and my sinful nature. Christ gives me the authority over all of them."

Positional Thinker's Action #2

"I rest in the victory already won by Jesus on the cross. By this act of God's grace I am justified, declared righteous and have eternal life and peace with God."

Positional Thinker's Action #3

"I believe that co-crucifixion is my 'death position' with Christ's death, which has broken the power of the sinful nature over me."

. . . that you may know the hope to which he has called you, the riches of his glorious inheritance in the saints, and his incomparably great power for us who believe. That power is like the working of his mighty strength, which he exerted in Christ when he raised him from the dead and seated him at his right hand in the heavenly realms. (Ephesians 1:18-20)

Therefore, since we have been justified through faith, we have peace with God through our Lord Jesus Christ. (Romans 5:1)

I have been crucified with Christ and I no longer live, but Christ lives in me. The life I live in the body, I live by faith in the Son of God, who loved me and gave himself for me. (Galatians 2:20)

Positional Thinker's Action #4

"I believe that co-resurrection is my 'risen life position' with Christ's resurrection, and I claim His resurrection power for strength through suffering and healing for my spirit, soul and body."

Positional Thinker's Action #5

"I am co-seated with Christ in the heavenly realms, where I am assured of victory as I actively engage in spiritual warfare against the world, the sinful nature and the devil."

Positional Thinker's Action #6

"I renounce the spirit of error and rebuke every spirit that doesn't acknowledge that Jesus Christ has come in the flesh. I will seek the guidance of a godly person who has the spiritual gift of discernment to help with demonic cases."

And God raised us up with Christ and seated us with him in the heavenly realms in Christ Jesus. (Ephesians 2:6)

And God raised us up with Christ and seated us with him in the heavenly realms in Christ Jesus. (Ephesians 2:6)

Dear friends, do not believe every spirit, but test the spirits to see whether they are from God, because many false prophets have gone out into the world. This is how you can recognize the Spirit of God: Every spirit that acknowledges that Jesus Christ has come in the flesh is from God, but every spirit that does not acknowledge Jesus is not from God. This is the spirit of the antichrist. (1 John 4:1-3)

Positional Thinker's Action #7

"I have taken the garment of praise, the shield of faith, the confident expectation of hope and the love of God to defeat destructive thoughts."

Positional Thinker's Action #8

"I wield the Word as a sword that penetrates the heart, pray the Bible and pray in the Spirit to replace destructive thoughts with the positive thoughts of God's powerful Word."

Positional Thinker's Action #9

"I am practicing positional thinking to prevent getting crushed under tough circumstances which results in a greater potential for physical, social, spiritual and psychological damage."

Worship the L*ORD in the splendor of his*
holiness;
tremble before him, all the earth. (Psalm 96:9)

. . . take the sword of the Spirit, which is the word of God. Pray at all times and on every occasion in the power of the Holy Spirit. Stay alert and be persistent in your prayers for all Christians everywhere. (Ephesians 6:17-18, NLT)

Since, then, you have been raised with Christ, set your hearts on things above, where Christ is seated at the right hand of God. Set your minds on things above, not on earthly things. For you died, and your life is now hidden with Christ in God. (Colossians 3:1-3)

Positional Thinker's Action #10

"To overcome the potential for greater physical damage, I trust in the supernatural healing power of God to supplement my doctor's treatments and will use the six warfare weapons to rout destructive thinking."

Positional Thinker's Action #11

"To overcome the social damage that comes from rejection and loneliness, I will not allow my sinful-nature thinking to convince me to isolate myself from others, but will be strong in the Lord and rest in God's acceptance of me."

Positional Thinker's Action #12

"To overcome spiritual damage, I trust in the sovereignty of God to keep Satan from dimming my heavenly realms perspective by trying to keep me in the 'denial' and 'Why me, God?' mode."

He himself bore our sins in his body on the tree, so that we might die to sins and live for righteousness; by his wounds you have been healed. (1 Peter 2:24)

Finally, be strong in the Lord and in his mighty power. Put on the full armor of God so that you can take your stand against the devil's schemes. (Ephesians 6:10)

"For I know the plans I have for you," declares the LORD, "plans to prosper you and not to harm you, plans to give you hope and a future." (Jeremiah 29:11)

Positional Thinker's Action #13

"To overcome bitterness, poor personal worth, depression, anxiety, fear of the future and death, and loss of control, I will trust the Holy Spirit to fill and control me."

Do not get drunk on wine, which leads to debauchery. Instead, be filled with the Spirit. (Ephesians 5:18)

If you are interested in ordering a Leader's Guide or Positional Thinker's Cards for an adult Sunday school elective or support group, write:

Dr. John E. Packo
New Hope Ministries
407 Joann Lane
Miamisburg, OH 45342
or e-mail: jpacko@aol.com

Check out our website:
http://members.aol.com/jpacko